老城市

OLD CITY

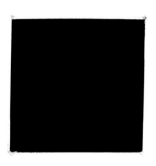

OLD BEIJING

People, Houses and Lifestyles

Text by Xu Chengbei

Text by:	Xu Chengbei
Photos by:	China Photo Archive
	Zhang Hongjie, Liu Zhen & Wang Jianhua
Translated by:	Huang Youyi & Cong Guoling
English text edited by:	Foster Stockwell
Edited by:	Lan Peijin

First edition 2001

Old Beijing
— People, Houses and Lifestyles

ISBN7-119-02837-5

© Foreign Languages Press
Published by Foreign Languages Press
24 Baiwanzhuang Road, Beijing 100037, China
Home Page: http://www.flp.com.cn
E-mail Addresses: info@flp.com.cn
           sales@flp.com.cn
Printed in the People's Republic of China

Preface

This volume entitled *Old Beijing -- People, Houses & Lifestyles* is the second book in my series *Old Beijing*. Compared with the first volume, titled *Old Beijing -- In the Shadow of Imperial Throne*, this one puts the emphasis on the ordinary people and divides the subject into more than twenty sections, in the manner of "a skilled butcher cutting up an ox carcass methodically and expertly." The culture of old Beijing is like a huge "ox" and the "cutting" should first and foremost strive to be accurate and then vivid. Though in most cases, the topics dealt with involve "hardware," I hope to also look closely at the "software" through study and appreciation. Originally I had a compact arrangement for the table of contents, but later I deliberately broke this into the small sections it has now. The purpose is to guide the reader through a kaleidoscope of aesthetic appreciation -- "shake" before you read each section and it will present an unexpected mosaic.

An apt description for the "hardware" in the culture in old Beijing is the phrase "too many." Then how were the relationships between each of the "hardwares" handled? Moreover, each piece of "hardware" had higher, middle and lower levels. So was each of these levels content where it was? Still more, among the many factors (such as economy, politics, military, law, culture and art) that kept Beijing under control, what was it that helped maintain its stability?

After careful consideration, I finally came to see that harmony in the sense of traditional philosophy was the factor at work in maintaining "relatively good relations" among the three aspects listed in the paragraph above. Often without having to resort to violence, harmony achieved through mediation and a gradual waiting process solved or partially alleviated most problems. Today, we are fortunate to be in the middle of a new era in which the social contradictions are quite different from those in the past and the solutions are also different. The experiences of old Beijing have been reflected at the end of the 20th century, thus shedding much light on our world today.

Simply significant!

I am more satisfied with this volume than with the previous one, but what will really be meaningful may possibly be the final volume *Old Beijing -- the Dawn of Change*.

Xu Chengbei
January 1999

Chapter 3 Men and Women

Chapter 4 Both Old and New

Chapter 1

Houses in the City

The Surprise of the Old Town

Beijing, compiled by Mr. Jiang Deming, is a collection of more than a hundred pieces of prose written by 74 authors about old Beijing from 1919 to 1949. The book was produced in Chinese by Joint Publishers.

It's been five years since I was last here.

After passing Fengtai, the train surprisingly gained speed like a snake in hot retreat from fire. I held my breath and was totally fascinated by the invisible strength of Beijing.

Beyond a patch of green, the old city wall of gray bricks was dimly visible, while rostrums with yellow glazed tiles and vermilion walls stood prominently among the rolling waves of green tree leaves?

This is how Sun Fuxi, a prose writer in the 1920s, began his famous essay called "About Beijing." At the time, trains were already going in and out of the city through places where the city wall had been torn down. A train could go all the way to Qianmen before it halted to a stop. That is where the train station was.

Take note that when "the train surprisingly..." actually suggested that the author was "surprised." The

Finally a train was able to go through the ancient city wall in Beijing, which thus lost its "air of royal dignity."

author was a Beijinger who had been away from his hometown for just five years. And yet he was already "surprised" to this extent. What would happen to an old overseas Chinese who had been away from the motherland for 20 and even 30 years?

"The old city wall of gray bricks" and "rostrums with yellow glazed tiles and vermilion walls" reflected the kind of respect the Chinese people had for Beijing. The expressions both symbolize the imposing dignity of the imperial system and testify to the solid and complete structure of the old city. One reason for being "surprised" was that the old city wall could not actually be broken open by the train and the second reason was that once when he got on a train, it was indeed much faster than riding into the city by a shoulder-carried sedan chair, a horse-drawn cart, or simply the back of a horse. This dual characteristic created contradictions in the hearts of those of the older generation, persons such as the author.

Cities in China have come a long way. When kings and emperors built their capitals, they generally took the terrain into consideration by placing their cities against hills and facing rivers. They did this in order to protect themselves from enemy attack. They used rammed earth to build defensive walls and surrounded these with ditches filled with water so as to prevent the

The city wall represented the dignity of the imperial system. When you see the magnificent rostrums on the city wall in the morning glow while traveling on a train, how can you fail but be overwhelmed with a sense of respect and fear?

Rails go through the heart of Chongwenmen Gate.

onslaught of enemy troops. As a result, city moats became popular and essential. In the past the criteria for judging the degree of safety for any city was first to determine how solid and complete the city wall was. Once the tall and solid city walls were completed, there had to be rostrums and city gates to facilitate the commerce of the people inside and to block the enemy outside or to "trap the dogs inside and then beat them."

Chaoyangmen Gate in the final years of the Qing Dynasty.

"Sunlight melts the snow at the corner of the city wall, revealing a section of dilapidated wall - - a gift from history! The years gave birth to giants who built and wrote history, and sent forth destructors of history, too. In the course of upheavals, the city wall was butchered and shot at on behalf of the residents. What fate does it have for its future? No one can see for sure?" This is how author Xiao Qian described his feelings for the ancient city of Beijing, called Peiping at the time he wrote, in 1932.

The city walls of Beijing witnessed many heroic deaths and gave rise to many thought-provoking stories. Emperor Yingzong of the Ming Dynasty, who was on the throne from 1436 to 1449, fought a fierce battle with the Mongols at a place called Tumupu. The result was the complete defeat of the Ming army. The Mongols arrested the emperor and then marched on to Beijing. Yu Qian, minister of defense for the Ming court, erected his battle camp outside the Deshengmen Gate in the northern part Beijing and fought what is remembered as a famous battle in defense of the city. It lasted for five days, and the defending Ming army won a decisive victory.

Over a hundred years later, Qing troops fought their way to the foot of the Beijing

city wall. Yuan Chonghuan, the viceroy of Hebei and Liaoning, was appointed to be the defending general. He refused to leave the battleground even after he had been struck in the chest by two arrows. The two armies were locked in a hand-to-hand combat and the invading Qing troops had to retreat in the end. Then when Li Zicheng, the leader of an uprising peasant army, took his force to a place near Beijing, Emperor Chongzhen (1628-44) of the Ming hanged himself from a tree on the Jingshan Hill. So the city was lost without putting

Deshengmen Gate, completed in 1439, went through a great deal as it was destroyed by earthquakes many times. Each time it was repaired. During the construction of the underground railway line in 1969, part of it was torn down. Now only the Jianlou Tower and part of the enclosure still stand.

The eight allied Western forces took over the Hall of Universal Clearance inside the Forbidden City.

Invaders occupied the Ming Tombs.

up a defense. At the end of the Qing Dynasty (1644-1911), the joint forces of the eight Western allies pushed into Beijing and the two empresses fled. The foreigners set up their camps right on the city wall itself.

In more recent times, the practical value of the city wall gradually diminished, but its beauty as a structure has become increasingly obvious. Thus the process of reconstructing the city wall or even the industrial technique for making the bricks is viewed as an element in preserving traditional Chinese culture. The city of Xi'an has the best-preserved city wall among the major cities of China, but it cannot compare with the original city wall in Beijing in terms of magnificence and significance. One reason for this is perhaps the fact that so many national tragedies took place on the city wall of Beijing.

The layout in old Beijing was characterized by thoroughfares that ran from north to south, while the city today opens from east to west. Which is better?

Emperors lived in palaces that faced south. Behind the throne was a screen. Further behind the palace hall was the Jingshan Hill, a "man-made hill serving as a screen." And north of the hill was the northern section of the inner city wall which served as the largest screen. With these three screens located behind the emperor, a city layout was developed that accentuated the awesome worship of the city wall and the "link-up of the north and south."

Changes of the old layout took place in the 1950s. First, the three city gates in front of the Tiananmen rostrum were torn down and Chang'an Avenue was extended both eastward and westward, expanding the boundary of the city. As middle school students in the 1950s, we took part in the holiday parade held every May Day and National Day (October 1) by walking from Dongdan against the rising sun and then marching in front of Tiananmen, singing at the tops of our voices. It can be said that Chang'an Avenue was "paved" with our footprints. Today, another east-west thoroughfare -- Ping'an Street -- has been built, making the entry into urban Beijing from both the east and west unprecedentedly quick and smooth. What is now gone is the symmetrical layout with the north-south axle as the center and buildings standing parallel to the streets along east and west. From the perspective of architectural aesthetics for the people in the East, these measures have

Beijing after a snowfall.

In 1553, an outer city was built around Beijing as shown by this southeast corner tower on the outer city wall.

resulted in many "losses." But the old culture in which the principle was to "benefit oneself at the expense of neighbors" has been done away with. This undesirable philosophy and practice of "to benefit oneself at the expense of neighbors" had long-standing roots in the hearts of many people in China. Is it not a good thing that this practice has been discarded thanks to the change in the layout of urban Beijing?

Which aspect of the two contradictions listed above is right? I am at a loss and do not have a clear solution.

North of Zhengyangmen was Damingmen (Great Ming Gate), which was eventually given the new name of Daqingmen (Great Qing Gate). The Revolution of 1911 brought it still another name: Zhonghuamen (China Gate). It was the first gate leading into the imperial palace.

The southeast corner of the inner city wall on which construction began in 1417, during the early Ming Dynasty, and was not completed until 1439. It is the only relatively well-preserved corner of the wall still standing in Beijing today. It has been repaired and actually looks much nicer than it does in this picture.

The painted beam in the residence of a prince.

Harmed by Love

In the heart of the inner district of Beijing is a large area of shiny yellow glazed tiles that lie across the roofs of the buildings of the Forbidden City. Scattered outside are small green patches here and there -- the green glazed tiles of houses originally owned by princes. Those living under the yellow glazed tiles loved those who lived under the green ones, for the emperors loved their brothers, sons, cousins and grandsons, many of whom had performed meritorious deeds by shedding their blood or even giving up their lives during the course of establishing and maintaining the rule of the Qing Dynasty.

Contending for the supreme imperial power, many of these people also fought against each other, killing whenever necessary. Those who eventually ascended the throne thought that, now they were in control of the court, they should try to reduce such losses from

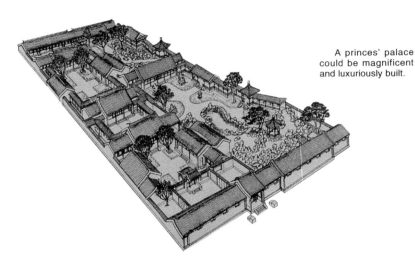

A princes' palace could be magnificent and luxuriously built.

Prince Gong's Palace, on Qianhai Xijie in Beijing, was owned by Yi Xin, the sixth son of Emperor Daoguang, who ruled from 1821 to 1850. Today it remains one of the best-preserved of the princes' palaces from the Qing Dynasty.

infighting and allow no room for their kin to nurture an ambition for imperial power. They arranged to have green glazed houses built so that those not on the throne could live comfortably, yet forget the days when they fought on horseback, and allow their muscles to go soft. Those under the green were reminded that above them were those under the yellow -- monarchs not to be disobeyed or resisted. And underneath both were the numerous ordinary people who lived in residences less pompous or even in quadrangle houses or the crammed compounds of the poor. The monarchs seemed to be saying: "I love you but you should not 'refuse a toast only to drink a forfeit'."

The residences of the princes were notorious as

Sedan-chair carriers at work as seen in this old sketch.

being places that were lonely and quiet. The women in these houses particularly had to bear extreme loneliness. In the cold winter, they longed for the spring so that on the winter solstice (toward the end of December) they would receive the uniformly printed "cold dispelling pictures" that were distributed to every room by a young eunuch. These pictures bore nine Chinese characters that meant: pavilion, front, overhanging, willow, precious, steady, waiting, spring and wind, written with big writing brushes. Each of the characters consisted of nine strokes and each stroke was drawn in outline form only. The women would fill in the blank space in one stroke as each day passed by. Once they had completely filled in a character, they knew that nine days (a

Gate of Prince Chun's Palace. It represents the highest class of gate that a princes' residence could have.

typical way of calculating winter according to traditions in China) had passed, and when all the nine characters were filled in, spring would arrive.

Along with the change of seasons, the women changed their manner of whiling away time. In the last month of the year (from late December or early January to the end of January, or sometimes early February) on the lunar calendar, the women members, led by the princess of each princes' palace, would prepare a particular kind of winter porridge with nuts, beans and rice. In autumn, when fresh crabs arrived on the market, the women would take turns hosting dinners. Those who ate quickly but did not manage to completely clean the meat from the crab shells would be penalized. And the "punishment" was that the woman would have to

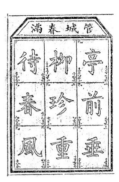

A "Picture for Dispelling Cold."

A view of the back garden in Prince Gong's Palace.

Residences of princes and their children, built under imperial decrees, had inter-linked courtyards in an architectural arrangement featuring seclusion and depth. The emperor meant that these meritorious people who had helped him found his dynastic rule should bury their ambitions and as- pirations and spend the rest of their lives in the quiet and spacious palaces.

take the others to watch a Peking opera. Such "games" were always the topics of endless chitchat.

The first generation of princes that came with the rise of the Qing were all very ambitious. They had fought for years in the service of the founding emperor and, once the Qing rule was established, they had been pulled out of "active service." At the beginning of the Qing Dynasty, the emperor gave the title of "iron-hat princes" to twelve people and each title was passed down by inheritance through the family. Other less prominent princes were lowered by one rank whenever a title was passed to the next generation.

The eunuchs in the palaces could have their apprentices succeed their positions, while the sons of servants in the palaces (especially cooks) could "inherit" the jobs of their fathers and continue to labor in

The elegant-looking theater housed in a provincial guild hall allows the audience to watch the stage from three sides. Upstairs, boxes were available. In the early days, men and women had to sit separately with men in the lower level and women upstairs.

A prince was leaving home on an outing. Princes who had fought on horseback for the founding of the dynasty now lived a life of ease and comfort, as they fooled around without any real work to do.

The position of a servant could also be hereditary. The four eunuchs in this picture (*from left to right*) were Yang Zizhen, Wang Fengchi, Liu Xingqiao and Zhang Haiting, who all served in the Hall of Preserving Heart in the Forbidden City.

the same palace. In the case of the servants, whenever a new generation took over, the skills went down one level, while on the part of the masters, each new generation was less ambitious and capable than the one that went before. I guess this arrangement did, on one hand, satisfy the vanity of the masters of the princes' palaces in carrying on the position as masters and, on the other, rulers of the court believed, along with the "degeneration" of the princes, that their imperial rule would be more stable.

Then what role did the princes' palaces play in maintaining the royal power? To put it briefly, there was very little any prince could do.

During my childhood, I learned this thought-provoking story from my visits to shows at temple fairs. According to this story, when the founding emperor of the Song Dynasty Zhao Kuangyin died, he was not succeeded by his young son as it should have been, but the son's uncle usurped the imperial power. The widowed empress took his son to reason it out with the son's uncle, now the new emperor. Though the emperor lost the argument, what was already done could not be undone. So both sides made some compromise. The uncle continued to sit on the throne, but his predecessor's son was made the crowned prince. The emperor gave him a gold sword with which the prince was given the power to directly go to the

Living in ease and comfort, the princes and princesses had to be content with doing no real service but in idling away their time in their luxurious palaces.

court without being barred by anyone, to reverse the decision of the ruler, if the latter really did something wrong. With the sword he could also condemn any treacherous official in court or hooligan in society. Thus the emperor and his subject and nephew struck a balance of power. Of course, under normal conditions, it was the sovereign who made all the decisions. However, if an unusual situation came up, the prince could "subdue" the emperor. This arrangement allowed the Song

Smoking opium removed whatever will and stamina the posterity of the royal family once had.

Princes and ministers discussing state affairs in the Emperor's Office of Military and Political Affairs.

court to solve a major crisis. It also gave the public (including spectators who saw the opera years later) an opportunity to let go their anger. So much was an opera story about how the royal family of the Song Dynasty solved their problem.

Emperors of the Qing Dynasty did not like to see

the princes involved in court affairs, nor did they like to see any court ministers and generals banding together so as to pose the danger of usurping power. They preferred that their kin do nothing and be not much interested in state affairs. They just wanted them to enjoy an affluent life. The monarchs loved their brothers, sons and cousins, but they loved their imperial power even more. They believed that if they offered wealth and a good life to their close relatives, that was the way to show their love for the country and nation. Never did they expect that these measures might produce resentment on the part of the people who once fought bravely and tenaciously on their behalf. The life the emperors provided for their princes eventually brought about the grave consequence of a total inability of the "eight-banner troops" to uphold the Qing Dynasty.

Thus, what began with love, ended in harm. Perhaps this was a result the founding Qing rulers did not anticipate?

Members and their families belonging to the "eight-banner army" had no decent job to do, fooled around to kill the time, yet lived in great comfort as they were well supplied by the imperial court. As a result, they degenerated into a "lost generation."

Intricate Alleys and Lanes

Ordinary residents in old Beijing followed a way of life that was handed down by their ancestors. Many flags had succeeded others to flutter in the sky of Beijing, but life remained much the same in the alleys and lanes. This picture shows the First Langfang Lane in the early days of the Republic (1911-49).

Years ago, Mr. Wang Zengqi and I came to the conclusion that people performing in the opera troupes were easy to satisfy. I explained that the old genera-tion of Peking opera singers mostly lived in a small community outside Xuanwumen Gate and that they had lived there for generations, as had their relatives and friends. Corner stores for their daily necessities were located there and even the theaters were clus-tered in the same area. The Peking opera performers could remain within a radius of several kilometers for months without any problems. Mr. Wang agreed with me, adding: "I once wrote an article under the title 'Cul-ture of the Alleys.' You may want to take a look at it." Before long, I found the article and this is what Mr. Wang had to say: "Beijingers are easily contented, for they do not have much demand for material things in their lives. They are satisfied if they have corn bread. If there are pickled turnips, it is good enough. And if they have the crispy kind of small pickled turnips, that is even better. A piece of preserved bean curd with a few drops of sesame oil is enough to welcome a daughter who has married and come home for a visit. And dried shrimps with Chinese cabbage? Oh, wow!"

This is a most apt and vivid description of old Beijing. To read it quickly is not right. You will need to read it slowly, find the rhythm in the lines and ponder each word. The words "Oh, wow" in the final line are most vivid. Have you by now digested the vividness and rhythm?

Beijingers were peculiar about the roads they walked on. As the streets and lanes in old Beijing were all quite straight, people could find no short-cuts to the places they went. Try as they might, they had to walk straight, making any turns at the

Mr. Wang Zengqi, a 20th century writer.

Lanes in Beijing were always as quiet and deserted as this one.

The layout in Beijing was clear-cut, as all the major streets and roads were very straight.

Crisscrossing lanes, small and narrow as they were, followed clear and straight directions.

The Inner Chongwenmen Street at the end of the Qing Dynasty (1644-1911).

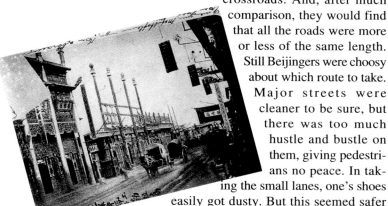

Old streets were the subjects of pictures foreigners printed and sold outside China.

crossroads. And, after much comparison, they would find that all the roads were more or less of the same length. Still Beijingers were choosy about which route to take. Major streets were cleaner to be sure, but there was too much hustle and bustle on them, giving pedestrians no peace. In taking the small lanes, one's shoes easily got dusty. But this seemed safer because one could turn away from the people and things one did not wish to see. Street names in Beijing were more meaningful and closer to daily life, unlike they were in many other cities where people named their streets after cities such as "Nanjing Road" or "Guangzhou Road." There were eleven lanes in Beijing named "Carrying Pole Lane" and there were ten named "Water Well Lane." In their daily lives, people could not escape from seven essential things and so there was also "Firewood Lane," "Rice Market Lane," "Oil Shop Lane," "Salt Store Lane," "Soy Sauce Shop Lane," "Mr. Zhang's Vinegar Lane" and "Tea Lane." Because people had to deal in their life with the five kinds of metal -- gold, silver, copper, iron and tin -- there was "Golden Thread Lane," "Silver Thread Lane," "Copper and Iron Mill Lane," "Iron Gate Lane" and "Tin Pulling Lane." One would certainly feel close to life when one walked on any of these lanes.

While walking on a lane, Beijingers would likely

stroll in the middle. That way, they felt free and intimate. Those who loved to walk on the lanes would not, in most cases, be high-ranking officials or men of great wealth. Beijingers were very cautious so that they would not overstep the lines or lose their sense of direction and location. The streets and lanes were straight so that people always were aware of the direction in which they were headed. And they knew clearly

and exactly where they were at any particular moment. In other words, they knew the distance between the center axle of the Forbidden City and their own location. It was the duty of an ordinary citizen to be cool-headed in this respect.

Tunjuan Lane after a snowfall.

During the last fifty years, Beijing has experienced speedy urban development and has expanded in size dozens of times. Tall buildings have risen one after another. This development, though impressive, has created a problem: what about the lanes? Old lanes are found in the old urban districts and whenever a large, new building goes up in such a district, many lanes have to disappear. In contrast, between the new buildings, many "lanes not called lanes" have appeared, with the sole function of allowing people to walk through the area. And their names are normally something like "The 3rd North Lane" or "The 2nd East Lane." What is missing here is the original culture of the

Jinyu, or Gold Fish Lane, where rickshaw pullers gathered to wait for customers while pedestrians walked with ease and leisure.

lanes that was characterized by the people living there, feeling happy and content with themselves. Quite the contrary, the kind of cultural mentality benefiting oneself at the expense of a neighbor, which was something very rare in the past, has now gained ground.

Living on a lane, one had many acquaintances who were mostly honest and sincere people. In a lane, it was very rare to find someone doing things for his own good at the expense of his neighbor. Such actions, however, are common along large streets. Along large streets there are many big offices and they compete in showing off their might and power. If you have something to discuss in the midst of such big offices, you have to do so through the exchange of documents, and if you want to see someone, you will have to first make an appointment. All of these formalities are need-

less in a lane where everybody knows everybody else. If you have something to say, just push the door open and walk inside the house. Then you can pat each other on the shoulder and chat.

This reminds me of the city layout during the Tang Dynasty (618-907). At that time, people were compelled to live in uniformly designed neighborhoods where each house was enclosed within high walls and shut up at night by a big door. There was no freedom for coming or going. Commercial activities were also restricted as the government established the east and west markets which had to follow orders in opening and closing at an appointed time. The Song Dynasty that followed the Tang abandoned such conventions, bringing in a period of great development in business and trade. The scenes of Song prosperity are vividly

Outside Chaoyang-men Gate at the end of the Qing Dynasty. From the top of the gate, one could see nothing but a gray and yellowish view which gave one a dry and desolate impression.

described in *Dreams of Prosperity in the East Capital.* After that time, one historical period led to another. Now all the high walls surrounding the residences have disappeared. But the mentality of wrongly treating a neighbor has replaced the old custom of being happy and content. Just exactly how can one explain this?

It has been several years since Mr. Wang Zengqi passed away. If he were aware of the recent changes, he would surely have some lines to add to his "Culture of the Alleys." Now what should I tell him?

Chang'an City during the Tang Dynasty (618-907). There were 14 streets running from east to west and 11 from north to south, cutting the city into 108 square sections as either living areas or commercial districts.

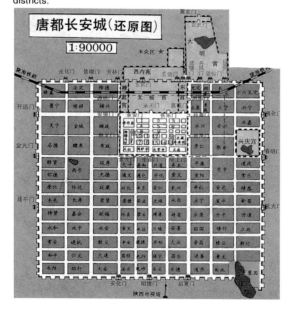

A local government office set up in a small lane.

Content with One's Own Place in a Quadrangle House

Quadrangle houses -- the kind of architectural arrangement under which old Beijingers lived from generation to generation. In south China, the compounds of ordinary residents were rather small while the quadrangle houses in Beijing, in contrast, were open and spacious with relatively independent rooms on all four sides looking into the central courtyard. Some of the better quadrangle houses had verandahs in front of the rooms to link them up.

The most prominent architectural feature of the imperial city in Beijing was its established pattern, with the Forbidden City under the yellow glazed tiles in the center surrounded by the palaces of the princes under green glazed tiles. Both the "yellow" and the "green" roofs had their proper place and, at the time, both "looked down" on the gray houses occupied by ordinary citizens. These spread out to all directions.

Ordinary houses in Beijing included two major categories: quadrangle houses and crowded multifamily compounds. Interpreted in today's language, the quadrangle houses were for the middle class, while the multifamily compounds were occupied by laboring people. In old Beijing, the differences between classes and social strata were clearly evident. When people were different, their houses were also different. The most popular thing to do in old Beijing, once someone

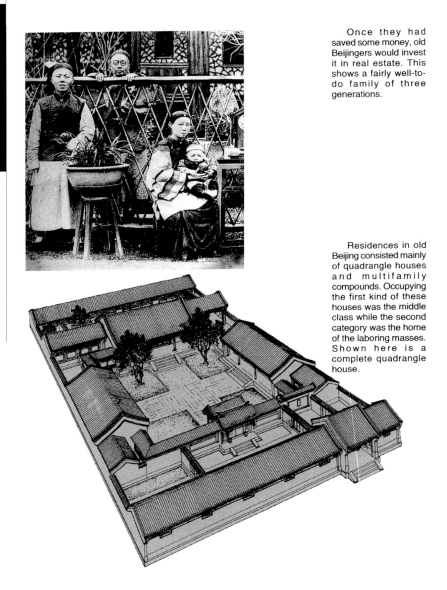

Once they had saved some money, old Beijingers would invest it in real estate. This shows a fairly well-to-do family of three generations.

Residences in old Beijing consisted mainly of quadrangle houses and multifamily compounds. Occupying the first kind of these houses was the middle class while the second category was the home of the laboring masses. Shown here is a complete quadrangle house.

In a quadrangle house, rooms enclosed the central courtyard. The main rooms had to face south. Another hard rule was "kitchen on the left and toilet on the right."

Straight crisscrossing streets and lanes cut Beijing into small blocks of communities. This is a gate leading to a house standing in one of these blocks.

had some money, was to buy a house to rent out so as to increase the "gray income," a practice then commonly referred to as "making earnings from tiles." Every month, the landlord would go, with proud steps and holding housing leases, to visit his tenants, family by family, and to collect the rents. The landlord probably did not live in the best house he owned. To rent the best house would, for one thing, bring him greater income and he would not have to show off his wealth. That was the philosophy of old Beijingers in regard to the housing issue.

The so-called quadrangle houses were so arranged that they enclosed a central courtyard and the owners were sure to be the occupants. They were the owners of all the rooms on the four sides as well as the owners of the courtyards and even the blue sky overhead. Inside a quadrangle house, they felt happy and secure.

Old Beijing was a very square city with most of the streets and lanes clearly laid out. These straight streets and lanes cut the urban districts into small square communities and the quadrangle houses stood on the sides of the "squares." The most ideal arrangement was to have the gate open to the south. If this proved

impossible, the owner would have to make do with his gate being open to the north.

The very room each member in the family occupied was a clear indication of that person's position and seniority. The best room sitting in the north and facing the south was reserved for the man and his wife of the oldest generation in the family. And the number of bays in the houses in the north could be three or five, but they had to have an odd number. The rooms in the east and facing west were also very important as they could serve as bedrooms and/or the dining room

Expensive quadrangle houses had more than one compound. An independent and large quadrangle house might have several interlinked smaller compounds of houses.

for the family. The dining room was another place that indicated the position and seniority of the family members and at the same time was a place where everyone could be treated equally. Unless someone was sick, meals would not be taken to the separate rooms. Another architectural rule for the quadrangle houses was

The rooms on the north in a quadrangle house were always the place for the man and his wife of the oldest generation in the family. The furnishings in such rooms were of high standard.

"kitchen on the left and toilet on the right." The family toilet had to sit in the east section of the house. Besides this, the rooms on the southern and western sides also served as bedrooms. If there were more than enough rooms for the bedrooms, some of them could serve as storage areas for odds and ends. In fact, it was never meant for all the rooms in a quadrangle house to be occupied as bedrooms and living rooms.

Furnishings for the northern rooms were the most expensive. On the wall in the central room that served

Quadrangle houses of wealthy people were always very spacious, complete with gardens for trees and flowers, ponds for fish, places for raising pet birds and man-made scenery featuring rockeries.

As-You-Wish Gate, the most common kind of gate to a house. Shown here is one of the smaller gates.

Old Beijingers loved to grow pomegranate trees because the fruit contains plenty of seeds -- symbolizing that people would have many children and the clan would continue to flourish.

as the family living room, there would be paintings and couplets. Against the central wall would be a long and narrow table, in front of which stood a square table flanked on each side by a wooden armchair. Against the partitions or pillars on both sides of the living room were two rows of chairs separated by tea tables. When there were guests, this was where they sat and were served tea. The arrangement in the living room was rather similar in the different quadrangle houses. Interior decoration in the other rooms, however, was left to the discretion of the occupants. One rule that applied to everybody was that they could not furnish their rooms in a more expensive fashion than was done in the northern rooms.

Expensive quadrangle houses had more than one compound. The southernmost compound would lead to the one next to it in the north and the second one further on led to the one in its north. If the southernmost compound served as a guest area, the second would be used as living quarters for the family. Verandahs could be built in front of each room for people to easily move from one room to another on rainy days without having to hold an umbrella.

Two-compound quadrangle houses were the most numerous, although there were also three-compound ones in old Beijing. What was rare were houses with more than four compounds, as restricted by the fact that the space between two parallel streets or lanes in Beijing was rather narrow. If a quadrangle house consisted of four compounds, then the wall in the last compound was sure to be standing on the edge of the next street.

The multifamily compounds were the mainstay of

houses for residents in old Beijing. Many of these compounds began as quadrangle houses, but had become rundown. As more rooms were added, the houses looked shabbier and eventually lost their former elegance. There was, of course, another possibility. A family first built a makeshift house in an open area and then other families followed suit and gradually a compound took shape, with irregularly laid out rooms.

Between the quadrangle houses and the multifamily compounds were what was called "independent compounds" -- compounds built with a room only on the north and south sides and linked by walls on the east and west. Some families living in multifamily compounds gradually became better off and felt that to continue living in the same place was a disgrace. Yet they could not afford a real quadrangle house. So they

Once a quadrangle house, this one has degenerated into a multifamily compound occupied by poor people engaged in different trades.

either bought or rented an independent compound as a transitional arrangement. Many people who performed on the stage lived in such houses. Some second-class or even third-class actors and actresses who made a living by accompanying leading actors and actresses originally lived in multifamily compounds where they enjoyed fairly good relationships with their neighbors. Once they could afford it, they gritted their teeth and bought an independent compound and then spent a great deal of money to decorate it so that outsiders could not help marveling at the house. There was a practical reason for this. When people came to Beijing from Shanghai to recruit actors and actresses, they would, before going into a house, take a close look at the kind of houses their candidates had. If a candidate had an independent house, he or she was in a position to ask for a "more generous" salary.

The Dragon Beard Ditch, a drama written by Lao She, a noted 20th century playwright and author, shows the hard life of laboring people at the bottom of the social strata in old Beijing. The story takes place in a multifamily compound.

Such stories testify to the fact that for generations in old Beijing, the house a person lived in told a great deal about that person. Then the question arises: were people living in different kinds of

houses antagonistic to each other? It would be wrong to say no, but antagonism was certainly not very intense.

A bird's eye look at the color and structure of the houses in Beijing reveals a sense of balance and tranquillity. The owners of the different houses were content with their own color as no one felt out of place or wanted to revolt against the color of others. To remain at one's own place was a characteristic common to old Beijingers who were living in different conditions. Day in and day out, they walked their straight way and few ever thought of straying from their own course or trying to change their position through improper means.

A side room in a quadrangle house.

This rickshaw puller made a living by his hard labor. He is depicted here waiting for his customer.

The Tonghui River was still visible before the railway came to Beijing. Later, boatmen gradually lost their businesses.

Finding the Water

When people were dredging a river in Tongzhou, in eastern suburban Beijing, in 1998, they discovered an ancient boat that was 17.5 meters long, dating from the Ming Dynasty (1368-1644). The discovery was proof that the development Beijing during the Ming Dynasty included inland navigation. In the Qing Dynasty that succeeded the Ming, the Tonghui River from Tongzhou to Beijing proper gradually silted up. And the network of waterways inside Beijing grew increasingly sparse as many rivers, streams or canals were filled up to become roads. This has resulted in the belief among many that Beijing has always been as dry as it is today.

When I was young, I could see Xianyukou -- Fresh Fish Entrance -- east of the street where I lived. I stretched my neck to look in that direction and wondered if there were fresh live fish there. But all I saw

was the coming and going of people, and this left me bewildered and puzzled. To me, street names should not cheat people. Wasn't Roushi -- Meat Market -- on the east side of the street outside Qianmen Gate a place where once meat was traded? Then where had the live fish gone? When I grew older, I was stranded by a sudden rain one summer day in Nanchizi Lane in the East District. The whole middle section of the street was soon submerged in water. But Beijing grew drier as I be-

Rippling water and plenty of boats. You may find it hard to believe this was true in Beijing in the 1930s.

When I was growing up, I found it difficult to walk through the knee-deep snow that used to fall.

The Zhengyang-men Rostrum after snow. The road is dirty with footprints and vehicle tire prints.

came older. The kind of snow that was knee deep when I was young has not been seen here for years now.

Once I read an article by Shen Congwen under the title "A Visit to the Second Sluice Gate" in which he wrote: "Go along the railway from Chongwenmen Gate to Dongbianmen Gate. And then follow the canal from there and you will soon arrive at the Second Sluice Gate." The Second Sluice Gate marked the section that extended westward from the Grand Canal after the latter reached Tongzhou all the way from south China. Boats carrying grain would dock at this place in order to unload. Mr. Shen learned this from some elderly people when he went to visit the sluice gate. The river gradually filled up and grain boats could no longer travel there. Thus the sluice gate fell into disuse. People who had the time and interest would still go on foot out of the city proper to look for the bygone scenery, which resulted in a "second round of prosperity" for the area, as many people stood on the dike as tourists. Clever kids would ask tourists to throw "silver dumplings" into the river water and they would jump in to catch the "silver dumplings" and hold them in their mouths as they played and enjoyed themselves in the river. This delighted the tourists on the dike.

It was not until many years later when I turned from my study of Peking opera to a study of the history of Beijing that I realized a surprising historical fact -- north China used to suffer a great deal from floods! Starting with the Eastern Han Dynasty (25-220), all the successive dynasties made efforts to dig canals on the North China Plain to control the water flow, an endeavor that, although guarantying the defense needs of the major strategic towns and imperial capital, resulted in the destruction of the river system of the North China Plain, as many rivers that originally fed

Tourists who came to the riverside for an outing.

The suburbs of Beijing used to be crisscrossed with rivers and canals.

directly into the sea were then blocked in the middle and diverted northward to the Haihe River. The consequence of this change was that whenever there was a heavy rain, the Haihe River would spill over its banks, flooding the areas along its sides. After the tenth century, in an effort to prevent the northern Liao army from marching southward, the Song court introduced a "lake and pond building policy" on the North China Plain that gave rise to a "great wall of water" which meandered for more than 400 kilometers. Water

Looking up from this height, you would see a dull sky. Looking down, you would see nothing but low houses shrouded in sand and dust. Desolate yellow was the dominant color of the scenery. Beijing, which used to suffer from floods has now dried up.

at certain sections was "as deep as three meters." Later when Dadu, as Beijing was called when it was the capital of the Yuan Dynasty, was being constructed, a major strategic shift was taken to abandon the Lianhua Lake water system, which had very little water, and to replace it with the more resourceful Gaoliang River water system. Because even this water system sometimes was not enough to ensure river transportation and farmland irrigation, Guo Shoujing, a noted specialist on water conservation during the Yuan Dynasty, opened up a new water source to bring water from the Shenshan Spring in Baifu Village, Changping, and to merge this with water stored at Yimu Spring and Jade Spring. This water was then channeled through Kunming Lake into the Gaoliang River. Further on, the water flowed through Lizhengmen and Wenmingmen into the Zhahe

After a snowfall, trees whose leaves had already fallen were laden with a layer of cloudy and misty snowflakes. The roofs of the rostrums in the city wall were crowned with white snow while their eaves hung with ice from melting snow. Looking around, you see a world of white snow.

Today's Fresh Fish Entrance Lane. To take a stroll there, you can still relive the dreams of the prosperity that this place used to enjoy as a fresh fish market.

River where the Second Sluice Gate was located. Twenty sluice gates were added between Tongzhou and Dadu, to be opened at calculated times so as to reduce the water drop caused by the rise and fall of the terrain, finally solving the difficulty in river transportation and partially solving the problem in farmland irrigation.

Not long ago, I once again found myself strolling along Fresh Fish Entrance Lane where the road is almost too narrow and too busy to walk through. By now I had learned that the Dazhong Theater in the lane was originally called the Huale Theater, in front of which a small river used to flow during the early years of the Qing Dynasty. To prove what I had learned, I visited a folklore specialist. Seeing that I was only half convinced, the old man rolled up his bedding to reveal a thick stack of paper. He spread it out and, to my surprise, it was a map from the reign of Emperor Qianlong (1736-95)! True indeed, a small river coming out of the city moat outside the Qianmen Gate meandered its way southeastward to pass by the Huale

A camel caravan on
the Marco Polo Bridge.

Theater!

It seemed my thoughts suddenly drifted into the sky of history and I could see people's hesitation in choosing this exact site for establishing the city of Beijing years ago.

The end of the Marco Polo Bridge, several dozen kilometers southwest of today's Beijing proper, was originally where three major roads converged (one from Shanxi to the west, one from northern Hebei in the north and another from the south). From a pure geographical point of view, this would have been the most ideal site on which to build the city. But as the decision was almost made, someone said: "This place will not do! When torrential rains fall in the upper reaches of the river, floods will come down along the Yongding River turning this place into a country of water!" Who was the man that made the remark? People turned around but the man had disappeared. Obviously it was a man of history who was pouring some enlightenment on the muddle-headed officials.

Dynasties came and went. Whenever a new power was established, it would become engaged in massive construction. Sometimes a new site had to be chosen so that the city would be built anew. Where would the timber come from? To ship it from far away was not as convenient as felling trees locally. The Western Hills to the west of Beijing used to be covered with thick forests and then, several dynasties later, they were turned into barren mountains.

For half a century, industry has made great headway in Beijing, increasingly consuming large quantities of water. Where does the water come from? Pumped from underground. The result is a drastic dropping of the water level underground and the complete "drying up" of the earth's surface.

What are the problems with having a shortage of water? In a restricted sense, people feel uncomfortable in their life. And in a broad sense, the city can no longer develop. Eventually the capital of the country will have to be relocated, leaving behind nothing but ruins.

If this really happens, it will not only be the ancestors that the Beijingers have let down.

Where is the lost water that old Beijing had plenty of to be found today?

To build the imperial palace, massive tree felling took place. As the majestic palace rose, the Western Hills, once home of thick forests, were turned bare, revealing grotesque rocks and barren valleys.

US troops as part of the eight Western allied forces parading in front of the Zhengyangmen Rostrum.

A painting by the hand of a foreign artist entitled: Chinese emperor receiving officials.

Emperor Guangxu returning from a ceremony offering sacrifices to the gods at the Temple of Heaven as his entourage passed by Zhengyangmen on way to the Forbidden City. The group was anything but being pompous. The guards could not even walk in unified steps. It was as if they were from a falling family. This symbolized the fall of the Qing Dynasty that would take place in a few years' time.

Beijing now suffers from a shortage of water. The city moat which used to be too wide to cross has very little water in this picture.

At the foot of the city wall by the city moat were many stores, shops and hotels.

Two grannies with a group of poor kids.

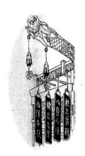
Chapter 2

Dreams of the Street

Signs introducing the "ten most famous medicines" in a traditional drug store.

Henian Hall; Tongren Hall

What are the charms of old drug stores?

Some people are attracted by their signboards. Take, for example, "Henian Hall", founded 400 years ago. It has a combination of thought-provoking vertical and horizontal signboards. Hanging in the center of the main room is a board announcing "Henian Hall" in the handwriting of the Ming Dynasty official Yan Song. Outside, another board says "West Henian Hall," and is said to bear the handwriting of Yan Shifan, the son of Yan Song. There are two accompanying boards. One carries the handwriting of a Ming Dynasty national hero named Qi Jiguang and the other has words written by Yang Jisheng, the man who brought a charge of ten serious crimes against Yan Song and introduced an impeachment against him. This arrangement does indeed arouse some thought. Yan Song and his son were notoriously vicious and treacherous officials, but that did not prevent them from being good at calligraphy. Loyal officials and treacherous officials were diametrically opposed to each other during their lifetimes, but as time passed, people customarily allowed the calligraphy work of a loyal official to stand next to that by a treacherous official out of aesthetic considerations.

Henian Hall was very close to Caishikou (Vegetable Market Entrance), the place that served as the execution ground during the Qing Dynasty. The execution officer was said to have sat in the entryway of this old drug store. Family members of those sentenced to death would bribe the execution officer so that he would do a quick and clean job in the hope that their men would suffer less. Once he chopped off the head of a man condemned

Yongren Hall Pharmacy of the Republican period (1911-49) was housed in a Western style building.

The grand-looking Nanqingren Hall Pharmacy had a facade that was rendered in an elegant and traditional architectural style.

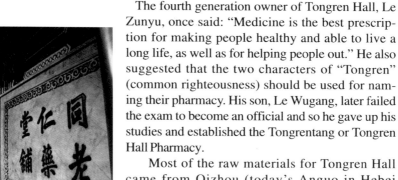

Tongren Hall Pharmacy, a hundred-year-old drug store on Dashilan Lane.

to death, he would quickly place a steamed bun where the cut was. Then those pharmacists at Henian Hall would use this bun with human blood on it to concoct some medicines.

The fourth generation owner of Tongren Hall, Le Zunyu, once said: "Medicine is the best prescription for making people healthy and able to live a long life, as well as for helping people out." He also suggested that the two characters of "Tongren" (common righteousness) should be used for naming their pharmacy. His son, Le Wugang, later failed the exam to become an official and so he gave up his studies and established the Tongrentang or Tongren Hall Pharmacy.

Most of the raw materials for Tongren Hall came from Qizhou (today's Anguo in Hebei Province) and Yingkou in Liaoning Province. The former was an entrepot of herbal medicinal materials while the latter was a trading center for tonic products meant for use in winter. Large temple fairs were held at fixed times in both places. Only after representatives of Tongren Hall arrived, did either of

these fairs officially begin to do business. The best herbs and tonic raw materials, such as ginseng and pilose antlers, were always reserved for Tongren Hall

At the east entrance of Dashilan Lane on which Tongren Hall sat was a sparkling copper archway erected by the pharmacy. On top of this were huge characters announcing the "Tongren Hall Pharmacy." Old Beijing was poorly lit at night. Tongren Hall thus hung a row of five red lanterns at the entrance

Rows of drawers and black jugs contained different ingredients of herbal medicine. Shop assistants worked in an orderly fashion, picking out the ingredients, weighing them and wrapping them up in separate packages. While they were working, the old store was permeated with the smell of medicines.

of many streets. Each lantern bore a character and five of them read "Tong Ren Tang Yao Dian," which formed the sign of the "Tongren Hall Pharmacy." While all of this is true, the greatest charm of the old drug stores lay in the mixing of their herbs. The shop assistants picked up a pinch here and a pinch there from rows of small drawers behind them. Could such things cure people of their ailments? What was the secret in the little copper weighing apparatus in the hand of the shop assistant? There were many different kinds of diseases, but the drug stores only had a few rows of drawers filled with medicinal ingredients. How come, when they added some of this and some of that, they had something effective against diseases? Wasn't this magic? It was really fascinating! Young as I was, I stood outside the high counter in the drug store thousands of times watching the shop assistants mixing herbal medicines in a composed and steady manner.

I was not alone. Years later when I learned to write Peking opera scripts for the China Peking Opera Troupe, I found that my teacher Fan Junhong was equally interested in and fascinated with medicines. During the late years of his life, Mr. Fan went so far as to study the "Concoction Song" of traditional Chinese medicine. He said: "The so-called 'Concoction Song' came from ages of clinical practice, the accumulation of treatment experiences and the collection of effective prescriptions. You can strictly follow the prescriptions or make some amendments. Because of the differences associated with the quality and variety of the medicinal ingredients, doctors must understand the functions of each herb and the interacting relations between them, while trying to be familiar with

The Yu's Pharmacy that was a wholesaler of traditional Chinese medicine.

the content of the 'Concoction Song.' Otherwise a doctor will not know what to add and what to take out. If he adds and takes out when he does not understand the functions and relations, the drugs he prescribes will not have the right kind of effect?" It seems the "Concoction Song" gave Mr. Fan a clue to understanding the interrelationships in the performing troupe and led to his success. Major drug store assistants never thought that, while carefully and dutifully trying to cure people of their diseases, they would also be shedding light on the understanding of a person in a Peking opera troupe.

The famous playwright Mr. Fan Junhong.

Guangsheng Pharmacy carried both Western and traditional Chinese medicines.

Romantic Teahouses

During my child-hood, I was not interested in keeping the company of adults who chatted and sipped tea in a teahouse. So I climbed onto a tree to while away the time. When my parents found out what I was doing, they invariably scolded me for what I had done.

When I was still young, all the teahouses had disappeared but tea stalls were still available. In the early 1950s, my mother took me to the West Woods in Zhongshan Park for tea. I saw that there were many rattan chairs around several tables in the open air where guests could order a pot of tea and stay as long as they wished. When mealtime came, they could order some dishes including pancakes stuffed with minced meat.

Several years later I went to senior high school and some of my classmates liked to write poems in the old style. It was a hobby we did not want to make known on campus so we went to a tea stall on the Jade Island in the Beihai Park, right behind the right dagoba. Few people went there to drink tea and so we became regular visitors. A pot of tea then cost 30 cents. Often we sat on the rocks facing the lake water, sipping tea and chatting. Before long a poem would be composed. It was during that time that the play *Teahouse* by Lao She began to be performed. We asked around and learned that in the Tianqiao area there were still some old teahouses. As we set out to visit one of these teahouses, we wondered: were teahouses the right places for high school students?

In the arms of my mother.

We learned from elderly people that Lao She's *Teahouse* was based on the Grand Teahouse which launched its business in the late years of the Qing Dynasty. When it was on the verge of closing

The teahouse on the Jade Island in the Beihai Park was where we, a group of high school students, often gathered.

The snap shot is of a scene from the drama *Teahouse* and the drawing shows the design of the stage. The Grand Teahouse, which for a while was so popular, looked exactly like what was portrayed in the drama.

down in 1900, the owner made a quick decision to split it into four smaller teahouses, each featuring a different theme: storytelling, pure tea drinking, wine selling and suburban life.

In a storytelling teahouse, customers enjoyed their

Performers offering the local style of singing in a storytelling teahouse.

Guan Xuezeng, a noted artist, performing *qinshu* -- a kind of folk art for storytelling through singing.

In a pure teahouse, all the customers had was their cup of tea.

Melon seeds and peanuts were also sold in a storytelling teahouse. Naturally the atmosphere in such a place was more lively.

tea while listening to stories told by storytellers who performed at the teahouse for a two-month season. The storytellers were known for their "sharp tongues," but listeners had even "sharper ears."

In the 1950s, I listened to the storytelling of *The Three Kingdoms* by Lian Kuoru from the radio, but I never had the chance to go to a teahouse and listen to him face to face, which almost became a great pity in my life.

In a pure teahouse, serving tea was the main business and this kind of teahouse provided a place for artists to look for jobs. I figured such places could be quite interesting but were too distant from what we students needed.

In a wine selling teahouse, the place of business was even smaller than a small inn. People went there

mostly for the purpose of having a good chat.

A suburban teahouse naturally would be located in a scenic spot outside the city proper, a place of a few low earthen houses with an awning of reed matting to shade off the sunshine in front of the rooms. Here people sat on seats built with bricks around brick or stone tables and received their tea from a terra-cotta teapot poured into rough, yellowish and sandy tea bowls. The tea was dark brown and tasted bitterly strong. To have a chat about the crop harvest with local farmers while listening to the singing of insects, frogs and birds offered one great enjoyment of the countryside.

By comparison, I was interested in the country-

Old Beijing had a large population of people of the Manchu ethnic minority -- the ethnic group that the Qing imperial families belonged to. Eating was one of their ways for killing time since they had nothing much to do. As the name implied, a wine selling teahouse also offered dishes and alcoholic drinks to customers. It was a more effective way to attract the wealth of Manchus who loved to eat and drink.

Earthen houses, reed-mat awnings, stone tables, earthen teapots and rough tea bowls gave countryside teahouses the in-toxicating flavor of the countryside.

Two women clad in typical Manchurian costumes, together with a little boy, enjoying a snack.

side teahouses most. Going on outings is my frequent activity of recent years. When I feel thirsty, how I wish that a few yards away there might be a teahouse with all the features of the countryside. Of course, it would have to sell tea rather than Coca Cola.

After making our separate ways over the years, some of the high school students in our poem-writing group have managed to reestablish contact and we now often get together. Those of us who had enjoyed tea in the Beihai Park particularly miss the times we sat on the rocks overlooking the lake. I can still remember

The back stage of a teahouse that offered artistic performances at the end of the Qing Dynasty. Such teahouses were known as opera teahouses in southern cities such as Nanjing and Shanghai. Customers came for the opera rather than for the tea. They watched the stage performance, sipped tea and chatted at the same time. Obviously such teahouses were very lively and noisy.

some of the lines I casually composed. For example in "Ascending the Height in the Beihai Park", my lines included: "While being busy, like a tree for a hundred years, the moment of tranquillity is most memorable."

All of this is away back in my memory, but some of the details are unforgettable.

I greatly miss the several rocks that protruded into the lake on Jade Island in the Beihai Park and the unforgettable times we had there.

Rows of shop signs outside Chaoyangmen Gate added much life to the old city.

The sign outside a copper ware store showed what the store carried.

Signs and Signboards

If you ask a young person about an old store with a long history, the answer you will get is often something like this: "Ah, yes I know, that is an 'old brand'." How can such an answer mean he really knows it? The expression "old brand" is not at all the same as an "old horizontal shop board." A minority of the old boards of shops and stores were written by famous people. The board bearing the name of the shop at the steamed dumpling place called Duyichu (The Only Place) outside Qianmen Gate was written

The horizontal board at the original Duyichu Restaurant was said to bear the handwriting of Emperor Qianlong, and the chair he once sat in is covered with a piece of yellow satin.

by Emperor Qianlong who had the writing sent to the shop by a eunuch accompanied by the royal musical band. An emperor was of course a famous person but such a board did not have much value. More often than not, a restaurant of long standing became well-known and so more and more people graced the place. And then one of the customers in the right circle or position would invite a calligrapher to write the name of the restaurant. The person who wrote the name for Quanjude (the famous Peking duck restaurant), for example, was merely a scholar who managed to pass only the county level exam during the Qing Dynasty. Such a scholar did not enjoy much social position, but Quanjude did not lose

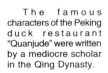

Words on the present horizontal board at the Duyichu Restaurant are in the handwriting of historian Guo Moruo (1892-1978). Where has the board with Emperor Qianlong's handwriting gone? No one knows.

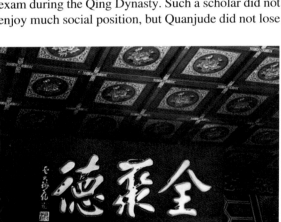

The famous characters of the Peking duck restaurant "Quanjude" were written by a mediocre scholar in the Qing Dynasty.

Shop signs in the commercial street at Qianmen fluttered like willows on a riverbank, presenting an interesting scene.

Though the horizontal board at the Liubiju Pickle Store carried no signature, it is believed to bear the handwriting of Yan Song, an infamous official of the Ming Dynasty.

its fame because of him.

Horizontal boards varied in value. Some of them were famous because of the person who wrote them. The name of the pickle store called Liubiju (Six-must Store) was in the handwriting of Yan Song, a treacherous official in the Ming Dynasty. His handwriting was "beautiful indeed," but the stories behind it were more interesting. According to one of them, Yan Song first wrote Liuxinju (Six-heart Store) as requested by the owners of the store (six people who put their money together and opened this business). After writing the name, Yan thought to himself, if the store was run by "six hearts," how could the owners co-operate closely with each other? So he added one stroke to the character meaning heart so that the name "Six-heart Store" became "Six-must Store." A second story has it that the pickle store began as a small wine

The handwriting of Lao She (1899-1966) announcing Imperial Cuisine Restaurant is still on the signboard of the restaurant today.

The Imperial Teahouse originally was housed at the Five-dragon Pavilions in the Beihai Park. Later it moved to the present location at Rippling Hall on the Jade Island, where they serve dinners of Manchurian-Han delicacies.

The signs from left to right unmistakably tell people the kinds of stores they represent: cooking oil and wine store, plaster store and hat store.

shop, but the wine was extremely good because the shop followed "six musts" -- six hard rules: Both rice and millet must be used; the leaven must be solid; the cleaning process must en-

In *Emperor Qianlong on a Southern Inspection Tour*, a painting completed in the Qing Dynasty, streets had all kinds of signs and shop boards, reflecting the prosperity of commerce at the time.

sure total hygiene; the ceramic containers must be of good quality, the fire used must be kept at the right degree and the spring water must be sweet.

Another example is Fangshan -- the Imperial Cuisine Restaurant that was opened after the Revolution of 1911 -- a movement that overthrew the Qing Dynasty. After the last emperor moved out of the Forbidden City and took up residence in Tianjin, several veteran cooks in the original imperial kitchen rented a house at the Five-dragon Pavilions inside the Beihai Park and opened the "Imperial Cuisine Teahouse" to sell snacks that used to be eaten in the Forbidden City so that they could make a living. As their business grew, they began to make all the dishes they were good at. In the 1950s, the restaurant moved to the Rippling Hall on the

The Ming Dynasty painting *Prosperity of the Imperial Capital* also shows the urban layout of the time.

Jade Island and took the new name of "Imperial Cuisine Restaurant." Who should be the one to write the name on the horizontal board for this restaurant? To have someone from the imperial family to write it would be all right, but it would not do any particular good for the business. So finally it was Lao She, the famous author, who was asked to write down the words for the board.

Horizontal boards are an historic legacy, but what preceded them were the shop signs and signboards that deserve more study. Shop signs and signboards already were depicted in the famous painting from the Song Dynasty *River Scene at the Clear and Bright Festival*, but the two of them were not exactly the same. Shop signs mostly indicated the category of commodities and the kinds of services as "trade symbols," while signboards mostly declared the name of the shops and stores as the "symbols of the individual shops." The former announced the commodities and services in their particular images, while signboards meant Chinese characters written on wooden boards, normally long and narrow. What is different between them were the size, number and style of words and the places on the boards where they were placed.

Shop signs and signboards gained their particular shape and style during

The sign outside Yijugong Silk and Foreign Cloth Store attracted business by announcing that "an extra foot" of the material was free to all customers.

Neiliansheng, a hundred-year-old store, was famous for formal boots worn in the court by officials, as well as cloth-sole shoes.

To attract business, the Neixinglong Shoe Store used both the horizontal board and shop signs.

Beautifully de-
signed signs for tea and
tobacco stores and tea
and pastry stores.

The sign outside a
comb shop looks really
interesting.

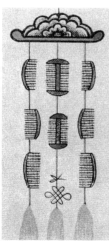

the Song Dynasty, but they were more varied and colorful in Beijing during the Ming and Qing periods.
Books and paintings from these periods portray vividly the busy scenes of the marketplace. *Shops and
Stores in Beijing* written at the end of the Qing
presented, in color, one hundred shops. This work is
very significant for the study of shop signs and
signboards.

In the contemporary period, traditional-style shop
signs and signboards were replaced by horizontal
boards, while modern commerce has made horizontal
boards obsolete. Instead, shops employ sophisticated
publicity signs, many of which use electric-light
features. The Quanjude Roast Duck Restaurant on
Qianmen Wai Street has erected a very eye-catching

sign over its archway facing the street. Signs crystallize the qualities of modern commercial enterprises. Through the new sign of a Peking duck, the Quanjude Group has brought itself up to date with the international market. More and greater efforts, however, are needed if people want to harmoniously combine traditional culture with modern concepts and thus plant in the hearts of their customers, in an eye-catching manner, what is available at the enterprises of Qianmen, a commercial center since ancient times.

Dashilan, outside Qianmen Gate, was crowded with shops and stores along the street. It remains a place tourists love to visit even today.

Vendors selling food in a lane in old Beijing. Longtime residents were able to tell what was being peddled when they heard the hawking of the vendors in the street.

"Have a Bite or Two"

Old Beijing had a great variety of local snacks. When people in the street felt hungry, they were accustomed to find a little stand and "have a bite."

What does this mean? Why not just "have a meal?" This was because the person was not really very hungry and so he wanted just to try a little of this and that for fun. Apart from the fact that the snacks at such stands did not cost much, they also added scenery to the old city.

Just who added what to whom? Well here are some examples for you to think over.

Yueshengzhai is a century-old store famous for its stewed beef and mutton. In the summer it attracted more customers, who mostly went into the store carrying an empty jug. Seeing a customer, the shop assistant would immediately say in greeting: "Sir, would you like beef or mutton?" If the customer cast his eye

Temple fairs were where people found the greatest variety of local snacks. When visiting temple fairs, people inevitably would find "a bite or two."

on the mutton, the shop assistant only had to ask the amount wanted before he cut a slice off the whole piece. Then he would wrap it up in a lotus leaf. Next, the shop assistant would take the jug from the customer and scoop up several ladles of mutton gravy. When the customer got home, he would cut the mutton into smaller pieces, cook some noodles to go with the gravy and then enjoy the meal under a big tree. Nothing could be more enjoyable. Even his neighbors would find their mouths watering. (Mouth-watering was in fact also an enjoyment.) So "a joyful sight" was created.

On hot summer days, sweet-sour plum juice was sold by the roadside. "Get me a bowl of the juice!" Hearing this request, the vendor would immediately scoop up a whole bowl of the juice for the customer.

A restaurant in old Beijing with a rather fancy facade.

"Stuffed sausage" was made with cornstarch and other ingredients. The sausages were cut into slices, deep-fried and then served with mashed garlic on a plate. People ate them with the help of small bamboo picks.

A two-bay liquor shop. One of the rooms had several large vats and the other was furnished with a counter from where the owner greeted his customers, always with a big smile.

The shiny red copper kettle for serving a Beijing snack made of millet or sorghum. The kettle was always a big attraction to customers.

At one sip, the customer would be able to tell whether the juice was made by "soaking" or "stewing." The juice made by "soaking" tasted better but took a longer time to prepare than that made from "stewing." Big or small, local snacks in Beijing all had their proper ways of preparation. Shoddy work and inferior materials would not produce the right taste. Substitution would never produce the same result. Xinyuanzhai on Liulichang Street was an old store for buying sweet-sour plum juice. Once a customer stepped into the store, the shop assistant, who probably knew the familiar face of the customer, would immediately greet him by saying: "Welcome, sir!" So saying, he would use the ladle made of bamboo to scoop the refreshing juice from a large blue and white ceramic jar, fill the

A stand selling sweet-sour plum juice.

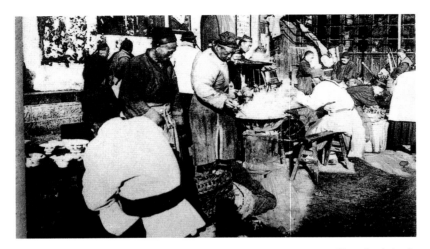

Warm food stands
selling noodles,
dumplings and deep-
fried bean curd soups.
Obviously they also
enjoyed a brisk
business.

bowl to the brim and hand it carefully to the customer. Though popular in many cities, this particular kind of cold drink originated in Beijing, and that from Xinyuanzhai especially enjoyed a fine reputation. Today, the juice from Xinyuanzhai is bottled and sold in supermarkets where it continues to enjoy a brisk sale.

Outside Qianmen Gate were many food stands, but here I will only write about one that sold "stir-fried liver strips." This stand, located inside the Fresh Fish Entrance Lane, enjoyed a wide reputation even though it was rather small. Though named "stir-fried liver," the materials used for this snack were actually pig livers and pig intestines which were first marinated in soy sauce, stir-fried, and then seasoned with a mixture of cornstarch and water. The next-door neighbors to this store were the Huale and Guanghe theaters. When ac-

Soon after the opera began, bowl after bowl of "stir-fried livers," sending forth a delicious smell, were brought into the theater. Sometimes, the business continued even after the show was over.

tors and actresses were hungry, they often sent people out to "order a bowl of the stir-fried liver." And the store owner would always take the food personally to the back stage.

Jellied bean curd is one of the most ordinary local snacks in Beijing, but there used to be two particularly famous shops for this food. One was Ma's near the Drum Tower in the northern part of the city and the other was Bai's in Door Frame Lane at Dashilan, in the southern part of Beijing. They were the source of the phrase: "The southern Bai and northern Ma."

What needs to be mentioned finally is a kind of fermented drink made from the water used in grinding green beans, which old Beijingers love so much. Here is my experience. I first tried this drink when I visited a temple fair fifty years ago, but at the time it tasted so strange I could not swallow it. In the 1980s when I was working for the Beijing Peking Opera Troupe, I went along with some actors to try the drink. Though I found they enjoyed it greatly, I still could not gulp it down. Then two years ago Mr. Zhu Jiajin was invited to speak at the Beijing-style Storytelling House. I was among the large audience that turned out to hear him. At the end of his lecture, the host took Mr. Zhu and some of us to lunch in a Moslem restaurant across the street. The host politely asked Mr. Zhu to select and order the dishes and Mr. Zhu complied. He ordered some of the most common Moslem dishes including the fermented green bean drink, quick-stir-fried mutton with scallions and stir-fried bean curd. Perhaps, because I had just been introduced to Beijing culture in depth, I had the urge to try what was typical of old Beijing. This time I managed to "gulp down" the drink and surprisingly found it "not bad." Ever since then, drinks such as the fermented green bean drink were no longer obstacles to me. Thus, if you try things with the culture of Beijing in mind, you may find them agreeable.

The local snacks of Beijing were not something you would usually find in an old Beijing-style formal dinner. They tended to be somewhat "unnoticeable"

"Ba gao" cake was made of buckwheat flour. Cold bean flour jelly was cut into noodles and seasoned with sesame paste, vinegar, garlic juice and sesame oil. Peddlers went around the streets and lanes hawking these two kinds of snacks piled high on their push barrows.

A steamed dumpling store at the corner of a lane. The vendor put a large chopping board on a one-wheeled push barrow to serve as his stand. The stand was located there like this for years and the vendor and the residents became old acquaintances.

Stand selling ice cream made with traditional methods in old Beijing. The methods might be backward but the ice cream was a fashionable delicacy at the time.

and required rather simple materials to prepare, but the people who made them had to put all their efforts into the job and those who ate them also carefully studied them. Beijing snacks thus became a uniquely glorious part of the catering industry in the city. They were substantial and yet inexpensive. Moreover, they added much pleasure both in terms of folk customs and culture. People's behavior, once associated with these snacks, became part of culture. The more people tried them, the richer the culture became.

The Missing Couplet

Spring water flows out from underneath the Cold Spring Pavilion at Soul's Retreat Temple by West Lake in Hangzhou. Mrs. and Mrs. Yu Pingbo once came here with their daughter to study the couplets and compose some of their own while enjoying the scenery.

In the 1930s, when Mr. and Mrs. Yu Pingbo took their daughter on a visit to Hangzhou and stopped at the Cold Spring Pavilion by the Soul's Retreat Temple, they were greeted by a couplet in the pavilion that had these words: "Cold weather begins when cold comes; the mountain peak comes over from where it came from." The couplet bore no punctuation marks, suggesting it was a question that invited an answer from visitors. Each member of the family matched the couplet with their own version in trying for a reply to the question, and each believed their own version was better. Their daughter then said: "I would prefer something like this: 'Cold weather began when it began, the mountain peak came where it had come.' " Both the father and mother agreed that their daughter had the cleverest reply and this added much pleasure to their visit to the place.

Couplets in the imperial palaces heap ornate words of praise together to extol the merits of the rulers. Wordy as they were, they lacked real content.

Couplets composed by men of letters among the ordinary citizens often read poetically.

This couplet with words reading "A house of fortune and nobility; a courtyard of good luck and happiness" engraved on the door, is several generations old and its content describes the ideals and hopes of several generations.

Couplets were a special kind of decoration on old and traditional structures such as towers, halls and pavilions. They always took the form of two long lines, each placed beside the other, and they were written in beautiful handwriting. There were strict rules in regard to the responsive tone and rhythm of the words used. As there were many nicely built houses in old Beijing, couplets were commonplace there too. Reading couplets was easy to do in gardens and palace buildings in the city but many of the lines fell apart under close scrutiny, as many of them feigned elegance and adopted affected manners by heaping certain words and expressions together, to the disappointment of visitors.

If you pace slowly in lanes and streets, you may discover and read couplets dimly written on the doors of some old houses with such words as "Honesty will be carried on in the family; learning will flourish among future generations," despite the cracking and falling paint. In just a few words, the heart and mind of an old intellectual is revealed. During the first few hours of the New Year in the past, people could often read spring couplets freshly pasted by the owners of the houses on both sides of the doors. Those couplets that were engraved on the doors would stay where they were for years or even generations. Spring couplets pasted on New Year's eve had to be new, in paper and ink, to give people the impression that they were freshly written for the coming new year. Once the red color of the paper had faded under the sunshine, the house owner would scrape the couplets off using a broom and water.

It now suddenly comes to my mind that the pavilions on top of the Jingshan Hill, which commanded the highest point inside Beijing at the time, had no couplets. Stretching in a row from east to west, there are five pavilions with such names: Guangmiao (Viewing the Wonderful), Zhoushang (A Panoramic View), Wanchun (Eternal Spring), Fulan (An Overall View) and Jifang (View Collecting) pavilions. The Eternal Spring Pavilion, standing in the middle, is the highest. Since the path to climb the hill stretches from east to west, visitors often go through the Eternal Spring Pavilion no matter which way they climb the hill. The doors on all four sides of the pavilion are thus kept open all year round. Had there been some couplets on the pavilion to catch the attention of erudite visitors, the hill would have been more culturally attractive.

On second thought, the absence of couplets there is justifiable. From a geographical point of view, couplets on the highest point of Beijing would have highlighted the culture and life in the city. However, at the time, the hill only served as a backdrop, or a screen for the royal

The Jingshan Hill, also known as Coal Hill, was built from the debris of river silt. A court minister named it Longevity Hill but ordinary residents often referred to it as Coal Hill, simply because burned coal used to be piled at the foot of the hill.

The Eternal Spring Pavilion at the very top of the Jingshan Hill offers a panoramic view of the Forbidden City.

Looking west from the Eternal Spring Pavilion one can see the Overall View Pavilion and further west is Zhongnanhai -- the "Central-south Sea" -- where the present Chinese government offices are located.

throne. High as it was, it could only be a subordinate place. The hall housing the throne had to have couplets, but the Eternal Spring Pavilion did not have to have them.

Couplets of real value were found among the ordinary houses. Pillars in front of the stages in theaters, for example, provided the preconditions for couplets. In Guanghelou Theater, the couplet read:

"Learn from the royal ruler and his subjects, learn from father and son, learn from husband and wife, learn from friends, combine all stories of loyalty and righteousness, stage them in show after show, in an eternal drama; Whether rich and noble, poor and lowly, happy or sad, joyful or saddened, present all happiness and sorrows for a close scrutiny, to the delight of spectators."

Couplets, often rather philosophical, were found on the pillars in front of the stage in old theaters.

The Eternal Spring Pavilion on the Jingshan Hill.

A comparison of couplets in the Forbidden City and the Summer Palace with those in theaters would easily reveal some differences. The former feature meticulous composing of words but all the couplets belong to the imperial school in both ideas and style of writing, which means they are rather lifeless. The latter, on the other hand, came from the people and brought out the essence of operas and dramas. Such couplets are thought-provoking as spectators, apart from watching the operas, can also ponder over the their meaning.

In most cases, the ancient capital in China was built along an axle line with parallel buildings on both sides. Take old Beijing for example, there were many expressions describing this parallel idea: Ancestor temple on the left and altar to the god on the right; the civil officials on the left and military generals on the

When hung in the center of the stage, the couplet served as part of the backdrop.

right; men on the left and women on the right. In observing old Beijing from this tradition, I believe a couplet on the Jingshan Hill, the highest point of Beijing, would have been better.

You see, this is one of my rather traditional ideas.

People who are 40 to 50 or even older are all aware that their education began by learning how to write Chinese characters.

Couplets engraved on doors always conveyed the ideals, wishes and beliefs of the house owners. The words on both sides were parallel and well-written. Though mostly they were jargon used repeatedly, real literary creations were sometimes found there.

The door frame of a public bath also had this couplet: the first line on the right reads: "The water is heated and ready before the rooster crows" and the second line on the left says: "Swarming with customers when the sun rises." While the first line describes the attitude and quality of service, the second line suggests that the bath owner is rewarded for his good service.

A sedan chair to carry the bride to her new home. Over-elaborate formalities for traditional weddings were quite annoying. "To welcome the bride" was just one of the small episodes in the entire process.

Funerals and Weddings

Weddings in old Beijing were so over-elaborate and extravagant that the newlywed got lost in the process. Upon descending from the sedan chair after arriving at the home of her husband, the bride had to cross a basin of fire, and then be "shot three times by her husband with an arrow." In the bridal chamber, she had to sit next to her husband in front of the bed while someone brought her an uncooked dumpling with the question: "Is it raw?" The Chinese pronunciation for raw, "sheng," is here used as a homonym to symbolize the expression of "Yes, I'll be giving birth to children." And the bride had to reply shyly, "sheng," before members of her husband's family satisfactorily let her go. The practice of making fun of the new couple in their bridal chamber, for example, followed the custom of "ruleless games for three days" during which people younger than the couple could make dirty jokes over the bride.

Guards of honor for an old style wedding procession appeared rather listless and tired.

From the very beginning of matchmaking, the entire process followed the economic conditions and social positions of the two families. Whatever the feelings the young couple might have for one another was of no concern, even in the minds of their parents. Many customs were particularly discriminatory against women. For example, in the morning of the second day of the marriage of a Manchurian couple, the bride had to be "welcomed back to her parents' home" and mostly it was the mother of the bride who had to personally come for this purpose. When the mother arrived, she and relatives on both sides had to be shown to the bridal room to examine the proof of the bride's virginity by studying the bedding. If the examination proved no problem, both sides would be happy, but if there was a problem, both the bride and her maternal relatives would feel disgraced. The marriage customs of the Han people were more or less the same. In the dawn of the second day of the marriage, the bridegroom would report to his mother as to whether or not his bride was a virgin before the previous night. If yes, a servant would be sent to the bride's maternal home to announce the

A guard of honor at an old style wedding.

The procession to bring the bride from her maternal home to her husband's home sometimes could be very long with more than one sedan chair. During the Qing Dynasty, those who could afford it insisted on having five sedan chairs.

happy news. The servant would shout aloud before he entered the lane where the bride's home was, for the purpose of letting all the neighbors hear what he had to say. And the girl's family would feel very proud of themselves at the news. If the bridegroom came up with the proof that his wife was not a virgin, he of course would not send anyone out and would tear off the strip of red cloth that indicated a marriage had taken place from his doorway.

It seems that weddings in old Beijing were held just to let other people in on the event. From the very beginning of the whole affair, parents on both sides racked their brains to be sure that both families matched each other economically and socially. Furthermore, they always hoped that the other side would be "slightly higher" in position and "slightly better" in economic conditions. The opposite side should not be too much "better and higher" though, or that side would feel belittled. To strike this balance, the parents or even grandparents had to work hard in their calculations. The young couple to be wedded, however, had no right to be involved in the discussions at all. They were always put in a passive position.

Members of the senior generation at a traditional wedding. They always insisted on keeping everything under their control and would not tolerate any mishaps or oversight.

Old Beijingers not only made a great deal of the "red events" -- weddings -- but they were equally good at "white events" -- funerals. During my childhood, I often saw funeral processions parading through the street. Whether one was in the parade or among the spectators, nobody really cried. They were shedding tears simply for show, for satisfying their own pride. In the funeral procession, the people who "cried" actually "howled," strictly following an established tone in a professional manner.

In the past, old people regarded coffins as their "houses" in the underworld. Many successful people, who had worked hard all their lives, insisted on acquiring a "good house" in the last years of their life for the eventuality. Time and again, they

Tomb of Gai Jiaotian, a Peking opera actor.

would personally go to check out the timber for the making of their coffins and watch to make sure that the painters did a good job in painting the coffin. Gai Jiaotian, a noted Peking opera actor, put his savings during the first part of his life into repairing his houses and the savings in the latter half of his life into building his tomb. When friends from other cities came to visit him, he would take them to see his pre-built tomb and even personally explain how it was built. He would seek suggestions from his friends for improvements. Indeed a man of letters called Dai Bufan once suggested that Gai should have a kind of slim pine planted on his tomb so that the pine would immediately remind every visitor of Gai's acting as the hero of Wu Song in the opera *Beating the Tiger*.

When the body of a dead person was put in the coffin, the coffin had to be kept at his or her home for a certain period of time. Relatives of the dead would wear funeral costumes. The more rich and high-positioned visitors that came, the more proudly

Gai Jiaotian playing the role of Wu Song, a hero who single-handedly beat to death a man-hunting tiger.

the family of the deceased felt. To old Beijingers, the first morning sacrificial ceremony was the most important of all. According to the old custom, after the deceased had been in the underworld for three days, he or she would look toward the direction of his or her home from the Hometown Viewing Terrace. The family of the deceased, therefore, would hold

A traditional funeral involved a long list of procedures including people who attended the funeral taking a bath, kowtowing, keeping vigil and the funeral parade.

sacrificial ceremonies for three days so as to treat the dead to feasts. During the first morning sacrificial ceremony, paper horses, carts, chests and other objects were burned. Then a ceremony for offering food for the souls of the dead was staged by the monks who chanted and then offered invitations for the gathering to twenty kinds of persons in the underworld. Just imagine what an important event it was to invite all the souls of the deceased to the occasion for remembering the newly deceased. After this, the monks continued to chant and sing. When inviting the soul of a military general, the monk would have these words: "Your excellencies, the sworn generals, honest military officers who

A funeral parade.

On the day the deceased was to be buried, the family of the deceased hosted an elaborate dinner to thank relatives and friends who came to express their condolences. The memorial service was accompanied by a musical band. Children of the deceased kowtowed and women howled and wailed behind a curtain. Everything was conducted according to established rituals.

enjoy renowned reputation for defending the nation, are sincerely invited." After the spells to invite the souls of twenty kinds of people were read out, the monks would sing the "The True Words of the Skeleton." I did not really take part in any of such ceremonies, but words like these made me admire the imagination and creativeness of our forefathers who employed the power of art in order to reduce the menace of death. Since these words were nice and were sung in a melodious tone, I deeply believe that family members kneeling in the ceremonial hall would find their sorrow quickly disappeared. Perhaps even a sense of joy might well up in their hearts.

The funeral parade was the last chance for the family of the deceased to demonstrate their wealth and pomposity. Early in the morning, relatives and friends would arrive and the bearers of the coffins would go into the shed that housed the coffin to do the "rope tying." This must be explained in more detail because of its highly symbolic significance. No matter how

A funeral procession is passing through the city gate on its way to the cemetery.

heavy the coffin might be and how long a rope was needed, no tight knot was permitted. This was because when coffin bearers pulled the carrying poles off the rope after they arrived at the cemetery, the rope needed to remain one whole piece -- to be used for such a purpose next time. All the howling and wailing at the funeral, like the knot on the rope, soon disappeared like a mirage.

A funeral band.

Temple Fairs

On every market day, Changdian and Tianqiao swarmed with peddlers who set up their stands to sell everything from daily utensils and toys to local snacks.

The Temple of the White Dagoba, the Huguo Temple, the White Cloud Temple, Changdian Market and Tianqiao were renowned locations for temple fairs in old Beijing.

At the very thought of temple fairs, I seem to have returned to my childhood days, an age of no worries.

At that time when the bell to dismiss the second class in the afternoon sounded, half of the class rushed out, kicking their chairs aside and turning their desks over, as they heard someone shout something like "Let's go to temple fairs." Schools at the time kept strict campus order but students loved the freedom at the temple fair. Inside the fair, a visitor easily got lost in the crowd like a drop of water in the sea. Students had to follow each other closely or they would immediately find themselves on their own. Dozens of years later, I cannot help thinking that perhaps it was the "absence of order" at temple fairs that had, in reversal, created a

A shot of the temple fair at the White Cloud Temple during the Republican period (1911-49).

"sense of order" for each student in those days.

What did we see then? Peddlers hawked their goods, but visitors did not go there just to do shopping. Perhaps they went there to see the other people -- those who "were submerged in excitement without realizing it." Temple fairs were big gatherings of people. There were all kinds of peddlers while the visitors also came from all walks of life. If someone became an experienced temple fair visitor, he or she would easily acquire the ability to deal with society, for temple fairs were miniature examples of society.

On surface, peddlers were hundred percent "sellers", but actually they were "buyers" too. In order to make enough money to support themselves, they had to understand potential customers standing in front of them. Peddlers were mostly people of "neutral characteristics" and "tactful approaches" who were really

Diabolo made of bamboo sold by this peddler was a favorite toy for children.

The original Liulichang Street was relocated to the west in the suburbs of Beijing during the Qing Dynasty. On its former location was built Haiwangcun Park in 1917.

good at "getting things done". If you got to know all kinds of characters at temple fairs, you would benefit from the experience all the rest of your life. You can compare people with those you had met at temple fairs and you would find that despite superficial differences, there are striking similarities. So before you make a decision, you can ask yourself these questions—who I am? What do I do? Which level of my profession do I fit in? So much so you will be able to handle things before others can even understand the situation, simply because you had come through temple fairs and that you are as experienced and "sly" as the peddlers there.

Temple fairs offered a visitor many useful experiences, but they never were like those presented by secondary school teachers who read from a textbook verbatim. Temple fairs were indeed like "teachers, " but they were "teachers of more advanced levels," for they knew you loved playing and furthermore took

your age and sex into full consideration when they provided you with education. They gave you the freedom, allowed you to enjoy yourself to your heart's content and made you achieve everything in the process of "playing and having fun."

To those in high positions and of noble ranks, or to superstars in the opera performing circles, temple fairs also provided an opportunity for them to visit under a disguise and thus be freed from the trouble of being recognized by the ordinary people. They were busy and cautious in their lives without any time really belonging to themselves. Whatever they said might not be what they believed, but

Tianqiao was a cultural street where many theaters and cinemas could be found.

Sugarcoated haws on a stick more than a meter long, pinwheels of all colors that gave a crackling sound, kites of all sizes and shapes, along with many other things, were always favorites among Beijing residents, old and young.

This long painting represents the scenery at Tianqiao in olden times. Camels traveled here too.

they had to conform to the established rules and patterns. They did this passively and they insisted that others do the same. As time went by, such persons grew bored and found pretexts to go to the temple fairs without having to show their identity or to follow any special purposes. They came to seek a moment of relaxation. Here they could relive the dreams of their childhood or freely find out about various aspects of society. They roamed about aimlessly and would not

show their excitement even when they found something special. These people could be described as the "most disciplined" temple fair visitors.

I watched many folk art performances at temple fairs, all with themes of ancient stories focused on emperors and kings, scholars and beauties that were similar to the theater performances of Peking operas. Performers of folk art shows did not wear any kind of stage costume, but always held a Chinese folding fan which they used as a horse whip at one moment and a candle or a chopstick at the next. The fan would become whatever they wanted it to resemble. In viewing such performances, I learned many historic stories (which were not exactly the same as what the history books said). Meanwhile I also began to understand the rules for opera performances. If someone had been watching folk art performances for some time, they would find listening to and understanding Peking opera singing in a theater rather easy. I regarded the temple fairs as my "second classroom." Now, as I think of it, I find the expression "mobile classroom" an even more apt description.

Itinerant entertainers converged here to eke out a living.

In fact, in old Beijing, there were mobile peddlers and artists who had no fixed place of work and totally depended on temple fairs to sell what they had. They repeated their labor while roaming about and in repeating themselves improved their skills and aspired to higher levels of life and work. As visitors, we always chose the temple fairs nearest home. As for myself, I actually wondered about in temple fairs and then went to a higher level into the realm of Peking opera appreciation. And this trip of my lasted several decades, covering most of my lifetime. It was not until recently did I pull myself out of Peking opera studies and wondered into the research and writing of the culture in old Beijing.

Walking on stilts -- a performance at temple fairs.

Temple fairs were lively and the visitors moved about in a lively manner. Temple fairs allowed the visitor to learn and discover many things that were thought provoking.

As for the kind of temple fairs held these days during the Spring Festival, they lack the kind of liveliness of the past. The way things are now arranged in the fairs is very much like that in a state-owned department store, with the things of the same category heaped together. This leaves the visitor with no joy of finding the things themselves. In terms of merrymaking, children these days are made to work through an everlasting process of memorizing things mechanically. As a result, today's children, most of whom are single, learn very little about the common knowledge of history and the fickleness of human relationships. All they have is a classroom that never moves. The second classroom, which was mobile during my childhood, is but a faraway dream for these kids.

I miss old temple fairs and I miss the "mobile classroom."

A "carrying-pole opera" seen in a street in old Beijing.

Peepshows were an entertainment enjoyed by both children and adults. In this photo, the theme of the show happened to be foreign.

Beijing women clad in *qipao* skirts in front of a stand featuring wicker baskets and iron kettles.

ing - Native Street

A stand selling cloth and fur materials.

The street was deserted with few pedestrians after a snowfall. Only the dim jingling of bells tied to camels could be heard.

Peddlers selling sugar figurines tried to make a living from pedestrians and children.

Chapter 3
Men and Women

Guangde Tower --
an old Peking opera
theater outside
Qianmen Gate.

Swan Song in the Peking Opera House

A review of photos of Peking opera performances from the past gives one the impression that they came from ages ago. At the time, the stage for Peking opera performances always protruded into the audience so that people could watch the performers from three sides. The same was true for all the stages in the Summer Palace, in the Forbidden City and in the theaters outside Qianmen Gate.

The "environment" for an opera in the East and West is quite different. In the West, once the opera begins, the audience area immediately becomes dark while the stage is brightly lit. Obviously this creates a more realistic environment. The audience in the West is also very polite, keeping silent and "hiding" away their attitudes regarding the opera. In the case of Peking operas, particularly in the past, the situation was quite different. When the show began, the stage as

Imperial Theatre, Peking.   Theaterhalle im Kaiserpalast, Peking

In this stamp issued by a foreign country, the building on the left is an elegant structure serving as a Peking opera stage in the palace of the Qing court.

well as the audience was kept bright. The audience carried on with tea drinking and chatting, making on the spot comments about the show. While the opera was being performed on the stage, the audience itself also performed and both shows complimented and contrasted with each other. In a Peking opera, it was important for the audience to publicly voice their acclaim and praise -- not only could the voices be loud, but the attitude had to be genuine and sincere. The loud acclaim was made at the moment the action took place on the stage. This was because Peking opera spectators were passionately eager to show they were "insiders" to the art. The more favorable noises that an audience made, the more this encouraged the actors and actresses.

People of Western religions believe the concept of "sin" and feel that "sin" was committed even by their forefathers. And so to live (including to watch operas) is to atone for one's sins. In their spiritual life, the Chinese people, however, are much more relaxed. For them to watch operas is to have fun—and so they will cheer for whoever performer does better than others. In watching Peking opera, people put the emphasis on appraising the performing techniques and few ever try to link the theme of the operas with social evils. Even fewer opera goers ever find the need of criticizing themselves from watching operas.

To look in retrospect at Peking opera at the turn of the century can overwhelm people. The period from

In an indoor palace theater during the Qing Dynasty, the stage had two doors for entry and exit of the actors in the opera. The left door was for the "entry" and the right for the "exit." The theater was lit with gas lamps.

the end of the Qing Dynasty to the 1930s was regarded as the age of old Peking operas. After the breakout of the War of Resistance Against Japanese Aggression in 1937, "not a single school desk could find a quiet spot in the entire north China." Peking opera, however, single-handedly stumbled forward for a pretty long time during this time of befuddled life for many people.

Shufang House in Chonghua Palace in the Forbidden City was where the royal family watched operas during the Qing Dynasty.

For several decades, those in the Peking opera circles worked diligently to improve their performing skills. Here I will not cite the most famous "four male superstars who played the roles of female characters" nor the most famous "four superstars who played the roles of male characters," but I will select at random three actors who played the roles of "male characters with dark painted faces." The generally accepted order of importance of the four major roles in Peking opera goes like this: male role, female role, painted-face role and comic role. But in individual troupes, the role of a middle-aged or old gentleman and the female role acted by an actress are considered the most important. A martial role comes third and the painted-face role has to settle for the fourth place.

Huang Runpu (1845-1916) was the third child in his family and hence he was given the nickname Huang the Third. At that time, male and female roles for actors were plentiful and those who were good at enacting male characters with painted faces only played the least important roles. He, however, was never dejected by this. Instead, he kept absorbing nutritious elements and good points from life, bit by bit. Often he obtained ideas from leisure activities and then, during a performance, applied these so that his acting was exceptionally quick and smooth, winning "housebreaking" acclaim from the audience.

The second example is Hao Shouchen (1886-1961), who was an apprentice of Huang Runpu. Mr. Hao was also a man extremely dedicated to the art of performing. He was so dedicated to his art that he no longer slept with his wife after he reached the age of forty. He would only agree to perform the following day after he was prepaid at his home by the man who arranged the show.

The small stage in Shufang House, which was part of the Chonghua Palace in the Forbidden City.

He was strict in regard to others but equally strict with himself. Finally, during the prime of his artistic life, he was given top billing among the famous male role

actors, which was exceptional for painted face performers.

Stage photos of Huang Runpu (*left*) and Hao Shouchen (*right*).

The third example is Yuan Shihai (born in 1916) who learned the art of performing Peking opera from Hao Shouchen. Before the two formally established their teacher-student relationship, they had an interesting conversation. Hao said to the young man named Yuan: "You ask me to be your teacher, but do you intend to break 'me' into pieces and transform me into 'you' or do you plan to break 'you' into pieces and reshape them into 'me'?" Dumbfounded by the question, Yuan replied, "Of course, I will break 'me' into pieces and reshape them into 'you'!" Hearing this, Hao broke into a smile, saying, "Don't be foolish, my child. The audience knows you're called Yuan Shihai, so when you study with me, you should try your best to break 'me' into pieces and transform them into 'you'!" Yuan remembered these words during the next several decades and has become most earnest in his acting. Later he vividly summed up his experiences of enacting the three heroes of Cao Cao, Lord of Chu and Zhang Dingbian. Although all three heroes were presented as men who "wore robes with patterns of snakes" (meaning people of ministerial levels in the imperial court) and of "high social positions," the differences in their official titles and personal experiences led to differences in the beating of the musical instruments marking their appearance on the stage and the way they moved about

Yuan Shihai enacts the role of the gallant and hot-tempered Zhang Fei, a major figure of the Three-kingdom Period in the opera *Reed Marshland.*

Cao Cao on the stage was quite different from the real man in history.

It was customary for the royal court during the Qing Dynasty to ask Peking opera troupes to perform in the palace. *Lotus Lake* was a favorite opera of Empress Dowager Ci Xi. The two most important roles were enacted by Yang Xiaolou and Wang Fengqing. The actor in this photo is Yang Xiaolou.

on the stage.

Not long ago, he performed in a multi-episode TV program of Peking opera entitled *Cao Cao* in which he put together the acts involving Cao Cao from the original opera called *Fighting at Chibi*. Once the program was aired, acclaims and praises poured in.

In their performing lives, all the three actors played countless numbers of characters on the stage, but without exception, once they became middle aged, all of them at one point or another portrayed Cao Cao, an important historical figure of the Three-kingdom Pe-

Wang Fengqing in
Lotus Lake.

riod from 220 to 280. Mesmerized by their performances, old Peking opera fans fondly referred to these three actors as "living Cao Caos."

Like these three, countless numbers of other Peking opera actors and actresses have devoted their entire lives to the art, concentrating on improving themselves, refusing to be distracted by other things, and fulfilling the historic mission they chose for themselves. Their work has added brilliant pages to the glory of traditional culture.

Theaters in contemporary times have introduced interior arrangements from Europe and North America. Here even the sculpture decorations follow a European pattern.

In an old style theater, the audience sat on hard benches. Of course these were by no means as comfortable as sitting on sofas.

Two little opera fans enjoying themselves.

The middle-aged Mr. Xun Huisheng in casual wear.

The Rise and Fall of the Xuns

In Beijing, there are many old residences whose owners used to be eminent people in the military, politics, finance, education or just about any other field. Unfortunately once those who had created their glory deceased, many of the houses fell into disarray. Telling about the former glory of such residents has become one of the most proud and satisfying things that can be discussed among the descendants of these prominent individuals.

Zhang Weijun was the wife of Xun Huisheng, one of the most famous Peking opera actors who played female roles on the stage. I came to know her in the last years of her life. Whenever I visited her at the house of the Xuns on Shanxi Street, Xuanwu District, I was warmly received and asked to have a conversation with her. Each time, I sat quietly on the sofa in her living room, listening to her monologue. At the time, she was in poor health and, as if she was anticipating what would eventually happen to her, she wanted to tell me the most important incidents in her life.

She told me this story. When Mr. Xun was at the height of his performing life, she and many young women were

Zhang Weijun, wife of Mr. Xun Huisheng.

totally attracted to him and even vied with each other in order to marry him. To her disappointment, Mr. Xun "already had somebody with him" and so she had to marry another man. After her marriage, she continued to go to watch Mr. Xun's operas and even deliberately rode her bicycle to work every morning by a route that would pass in front of Mr. Xun's house. Mr. Xun lived in the first lane on the west side of Xidan. Every morning, at the fixed time, Mr. Xun would be standing in front of his house and so he watched her passing by on her bike. He would look at her and she would look at him. Sometimes, they smiled at each other by way of greeting, but most of the time they kept silent, for even if she wanted to, she could not bring herself to talk with him given her status of mind at the time. Several years later, "the person whom Mr. Xun had been with" left and Zhang Weijun was also divorced. So she finally came to live with Mr. Xun and stayed with him until his last days.

Zhang described their eyeing each other in the small lane in these words: "That lane was nothing extraordinary, but for Mr. Xun and myself, every gate, every broken section of the wall and even the broken bricks seemed adorable."

At the first glance, the Xuns' house had nothing special to distinguish it from many others, but after hearing Zhang Weijun's story, I immediately felt a lot more favorable towards it.

According to Zhang, she loved to cultivate flowers while Mr. Xun liked to plant trees. Mr. Xun himself once had these comments about the differences between flowers and trees: "People are delighted once flowers blossom, but flowers cannot bloom for a hundred days. Trees are different in that they not only blossom but also bear fruit. Even when fall causes the leaves to drop from the trees, they do not give people a sad feeling, because people know that the tree will blossom and grow thick branches next spring."

Precisely for this reason, Mr. Xun enthusiastically

The residence of Mr. Xun Huisheng. An ordinary house in an ordinary lane and the corroded brick walls give the place a desolate look, but it once was a place of cozy and intimate life.

Xun Huisheng (*2nd right*) playing the part of Mrs. Lin in *Fragrant Belt*.

planted and took good care of the trees, making this an important household chore form himself. He planted over forty trees including pears, pomegranates, dates, apricots, plums, hawthorns, apples and crabapples. He personally did every job related to them from pruning, to spreading pesticides, watering and applying fertilizer. His hobby even led him to brightly polish the tools and neatly arrange them in a little warehouse. Though he shed a lot of perspiration in growing the trees, he did not keep all the fruit but happily distributed it to others, which was perhaps a fine tradition that had been handed down by his ancestors who were farmers. The dates in Mr. Xun's house were sweet and crispy. When they were harvested, he put them in baskets and gave them to friends such as Mei Lanfang, Tian Han, Lao She and Ouyang Yuqian. In the main courtyard, there were several pomegranate trees whose fruits were always left on the trees instead of being harvested when the leaves fell. The red fruits against the clear blue sky presented a charming view. Whenever a guest came to visit on the coldest days of winter, Mr. Xun only had to raise one finger and his family would know what to do: take a bamboo stick and knock down a pomegranate from the tree, now so frozen that it was as heavy as a chunk of iron. Then the fruit was put in cold water to defrost it, washed clean and put onto a blue-and-white ceramic plate so that the guest could enjoy this icy fruit that was by then as sweet as "a bowl of honey."

Though an avid tree lover, Mr. Xun did not reject all flowers. In his home there were few kinds of tender flowers, but there were plenty of fragrant plantain lilies, a blossom known for its quality of being easy to cultivate and eager to please its owner. This flower grows in shaded places. So if a few seeds were sown in front of a house facing the north or under the shade of a tree, the plant would soon prosper. In winter, this flower does not have to be moved into a green house, but it stands proudly in the open air, despising the cold wind and wintry snow. When spring comes again, where there was only one plant the year before there will be a patch of fresh plants of that flower.

Mr. Xun with his daughter Linglai.

Mr. Xun's attitude toward flowers and trees had something to do with his philosophy of life. He often said these words to himself and his family: "If you love something and want to do something, you have to first be clear as to why. And when you do it, you should not overdo it. Otherwise you will not only make yourself a nuisance, but you will also cause trouble and may even end up losing all your standing and reputation."

The flames of the "cultural revolution" swept the country in 1966. On August 23, some three hundred noted figures in literary and art circles were publicly humiliated at the Confucian Temple in Beijing. Peking opera costumes were burned and leading actors and actresses were made to kneel in front of the ashes. The Red Guards wielded the leather belts and spears and swords, used as props on the stage, to beat the artists and actors and lash them on their backs. When he went home from this humiliating torture, Mr.

Xun was severely bruised. His shirt, which had been torn into bloody strips by the lashing and whipping, stuck to his body and was hard to peel off. Stopping his wife and daughter from their sobbing, Mr. Xun said. "Whenever they beat me with sticks, I used my experience in deep breathing and exertion of strength to ward off the blows. Though my skin and flesh suffered, my inner organs were all right. But I really found it heartbreaking to see Lao She, such a physically weak and hard-willed writer, being given the worst beating and humiliation. What I'm really afraid of is what will happen to him if he cannot take it any longer?"

The living room of Mr. Xun's former residence. After his death, it was turned into a mourning hall. The interior decorations and furniture reflect the character of the former occupant.

Things turned out the way he feared. The following morning, Lao She drowned himself at Taiping Lake. Before Mr. Xun had recovered from the shock of Lao She's death, he suddenly found that a young peach tree he had recently planted outside the east window had one branch broken off by the Red Guards the previous day when they came to search his house. He gave a long sigh and said nothing for a long time. Later he said to his wife, "Go and find some strips of cloth and use mud to bind up the broken branch. Perhaps it will regain its life."

The original site of the Glorious Spring Society established by Mr. Shang Xiaoyun, who was also a noted actor who specialized in female roles in Peking opera. This picture was taken before 1966 and the house has since been demolished.

The peach tree did come to life again, but Mr. Xun died at the end of 1968. In March the following year, a rare hailstorm pelted the trees. A young crabapple tree in the courtyard quickly recovered after the injury from the hailstorm and even bore fruit that year. The older trees, however, never recovered from the disaster. Seeing this, Zhang Weijun said to herself, "Saplings are as youthful as young people. They have a strong resistance against disasters and are able to revive again, but old trees are just like my husband. They died and never came to life again!" At the time we talked, only five trees could still be found in the main courtyard: three date trees and two pomegranate trees. In keeping with past practice, Zhang Weijun took the fruit every fall to disciples of Mr. Xun and other friends in the Peking opera circle. Now she had no desire to cultivate any more flowers, except for the fragrant plantain lily.

After Zhang Weijun's death a few years ago, the residence of the Xuns was locked up. The main court-yard is virtually empty, but the fragrant plantain lily still grows lushly and beautifully in the four flower beds. When they blossom, there is always some descendant in the Xun family who opens the door to the residence, picks some of the flowers along with a few green leaves and gingerly puts them in front of the picture of Mr. Xun that hangs in the living room.

The four most famous Peking opera actors playing female roles, who dominated the Chinese theater for more than half a century: Mei Lanfang (*center back*), Cheng Yanqiu (*front*), Xun Huisheng (*1st right*) and Shang Xiaoyun (*1st left*).

Larger than Life

Ancient Chinese residences are a valuable cultural legacy for us today. The interior designs and furniture are as important and valuable as the architecture.

Upon hearing that Mr. Wang Shixiang, a master figure in the field of cultural relics, had moved into a new house, I went to visit him one cold winter day. During our conversation, he gave me a copy of his recently published *Chinese Gourds* and he autographed it for me. I took a quick look and could not help exclaiming silently, "Wow! There are so many different kinds of gourds cultivated in so many ways and each is designed to hold a different kind of singing insect!" Such unofficially published wisdom really deserves admiration. After a while, I got up and was ready to say goodbye, when suddenly the singing of one of the insects, similar to a katydid or a cricket, caught my attention. I looked around, thinking he might have the insect in his hand. Mr. Wang smiled and said, "The room is very warm and I do not have to hold it on me to make it warm. Look," he said, and then pointing to a

Cultural relics specialist Mr. Wang Shixiang.

basket of gourds, he told me, "Before you came, I was putting three kinds of earth into them." So saying, he picked up a small wooden pressing device that he used to make a slope in the earth. "This way, the cricket will feel comfortable in here and therefore sing beautifully." It suddenly occurred to me that I was really talking with a connoisseur pleasure seeker. Moreover, his playing led him to good learning and his bookshelf was laden with his own works, including *Ming Dynasty Furniture*, *A Companion of Crickets and Pigeon Whistles from Beijing*. The old man had accomplished something no one else had done in the past and few would do in the future. He had not only achieved a cultural distinction, but he had also given us many important writings.

Coming back from Mr. Wang's place, I began to read *Chinese Gourds* carefully. At one place, he wrote about his experience of being sent into a detention

Mr. Wang has published a series of works on traditional furniture in China.

house during the "cultural revolution." Even then he refused to give up what he had been trying to do, often trying to heal the wound in his heart by finding joy in objects of pleasure seeking. During those days, he often recalled the times in his childhood when he went to catch insects in winter. The memories were so strong that he would get up in the night and ride his bike to the Fragrance Hills in western suburban Beijing to catch a katydid, even though he was already over sixty years old at the time. He put himself into this mission wholeheartedly. Like human beings, katydids have both hearing and feeling senses, so they are "cunning and quick. When they hear a man walking, they turn mute and keep silent. Or when they see the shadow of a man, they will suddenly jump into the grass and flee. Their beautiful appearance and voices, however, make

In a valley outside the city of Beijing, Mr. Wang Shixiang is always able to find the joy of nature.

From emperor to commoner, the Chinese people in the past loved to seek pleasure from watching cricket fighting.

me totally attracted and bent to catching them. So I have to kneel or prostrate myself on the ground and wait patiently. Then they begin to sing again, in three to five quick and short notes at the beginning. They may stay where they are or move to another location. Still I will not move but I will wait until they become sure of their safety. Then they will begin to sing in long and long notes and loud voices, come out of hiding in the grass and climb onto bushes or trees. Feeling safe and sound on a tree branch, they will now proudly and bravely sing by quickly flashing their wings. Now I can get a good look at their location, take note of the sparseness or thickness of the foliage, plan how to approach them and how to use the net in my hand. Only then, will I act. Usually at such moments, I

Without other things to do, people enjoyed watching cricket fights on street corners.

take no notice of the thorns that stick into my flesh and cannot care less about any blood staining my clothes or socks. When I come back from the trip, I often find myself sitting by a light, picking out thorns one by one. When I try to catch an insect, I hold the net in my left hand and wear a glove on the right so as to quickly reach out toward the insect. Surprised, it will squarely fall into the net. At that moment, the hearts of both the katydid and myself are beating fast. The difference lies in the fact that I am happy while the insect is scared."

In the deserted mountain valley, the katydid and man are really equals. And Mr. Wang's writing reflects the spirit of union between man and nature. Here man certainly refers to Mr. Wang while nature includes the katydid as well as the mountain valley "which also has feelings and passions." I even toyed with the suggestion that Mr. Wang's descriptions of his experience be included into a Chinese textbook for high school students.

At the beginning of the "cultural revolution," all the wooden furniture that Mr. Wang had spent the early part of his life collecting was taken away. It was not returned to him until a much later time when the housing conditions had become quite crowded for him and his family. So he had to take the furniture apart, tie the pieces together and put them away. Afraid that the rebel Red Guard factions would come to ransack his

During the "cultural revolution," Mr. Wang's collection of Ming Dynasty furniture was taken away. Later it was returned to him. A few years ago, he donated his lifetime collection of traditional furniture to the Shanghai Museum, which has put it on display in a special exhibition hall.

house again, he plunged into writing a monogram on Ming-style furniture, which he worked on day and night. Finally he brought out the work that instantly won the acclaim of readers both in and outside China. Since then, he has embarked on a publishing spree and *Chinese Gourds* is just one of his writing achievements. A few years ago Mr. Wang donated his lifetime collection of furniture to the Shanghai Museum, which has put it in a special hall and opened this to the public.

What Mr. Wang has done proves this. An indi-

Kids with their pet birds.

Taking their birds to have some fresh air in the morning.

Imperial concubines viewing gold fish in the palace garden.

vidual cannot choose the "level of standard and importance" of his work and life, but he invariably has to take one of the two paths: living like a nobleman or that of an ordinary person, but in either case a person is not to be limited by the "level and size" of his post.

A Manchurian couple lived a comfortable life, really doing nothing all day long but whiling away their time in pleasure seeking. They still wore traditional Manchurian clothing.

Taking a picture of a chess match in front of a backdrop.

This stand sold products as they were being made.

Shop in Front of the Mill

People in the cultural circles in old Beijing had the habit of dining out in small restaurants. For example, when the host and guest were still in the middle of a cozy conversation, mealtime would come. The guest would then plan to leave because the host usually wouldn't have the proper things to invite him to a meal at home, so the host would invite the guest by pulling on the sleeve of his long gown. "Don't leave," the host might say. "Let's go out and eat in a small restaurant!" So the two would go out, take a few turns and came to a restaurant which might have only one room and just two or three tables. They would then sit down and the waiter, who would probably be no stranger to the host, would come forward and ask: "What would you like to have, Sir?" The only thing the host had to say with a wave of his hand was: "I'll leave it all to you." Then he might immediately call the waiter back and ask if the restaurant had "any special meat and vegetable dishes" for the day. The waiter would announce the list and the host and guest would ponder over it. Suddenly, either the guest or the host would say in a rather loud and sure voice: "Yes, I know what to have." He would then describe a rather creative recipe and the waiter would listen attentively, nodding his head now and then. In fact, on the other side of the partition was a pair of really attentive ears -- those of the cook.

The kitchen was just on the other side of the partition in this restaurant.

Soon the waiter would bring out the dish made according to the choice recipe suggested by the diner and would say in a respectful voice: "Sir, please try it and see if it is prepared the way you want." Both the guest and host would use the chopsticks to try the dish and then say: "Mm, not bad." They would continue to evaluate the dish for a time. At that moment, the

The owner of the Yueshengzhai Cooked Meat Store greeting a customer.

cook, who could no longer hold back his silence, would come out and stand in front the diners, wiping his hands on his apron and respectfully inviting help: "Look, please tell me how I should improve it?" What I am trying to tell you here is that after such a discussion, the small restaurant might have added one more house specialty to its menu.

This account is an apt description of the title to this section: Shop in Front of the Mill. If the dining room was too far away from the kitchen, there would not have been the experience of the diner and cook together creating a new recipe. Without the cook being able to hear the conversation, there would not be

Street outside Guangqumen Gate. The trend of having a shop in front of the mill quickly encroached upon the street.

the new dish.

Sure, the function of the shop in front of the mill was by no means limited to restaurants only. It was true of all trades and businesses. The street outside Qianmen Gate during the Qing Dynasty was very wide. The ample space gave rise to a series of small businesses operated by a husband and wife or father and son along the roadside. Gradually the stands were replaced by brick houses and later, a single brick room would be replaced by two rooms, with one facing the street and serving as the shop or store, while the one behind it serving as the workshop to process the products. The arrangement of the shop in front and the mill in back occupied at least a space as deep as two rooms. Moreover some space, at least another room deep and wide, had to be left as walkway in front of the shop. Soon the nice and wide street lost its width by six rooms of space. The loss in the width of the street, however, resulted in all kinds of practices and concepts associated with shops in front of mills.

When the scale of production and sale was not large, this arrangement was adequate and convenient for the business. For pastry stores, freshly baked food could be instantly taken from the mill to the counter. What customer would not want something fresh out of the oven with all its inviting smell? Besides, such businesses were mostly operated by only a few people such as a husband and wife or a father and

The smoking pipe hanging over the door indicates that this was a tobacco store.

The Qingfufang Candle Shop outside Xuanwumen Gate.

The Beijing branch of the nationwide Shengxifu Hat and Shoe Store.

his sons. These owners were both the producers and cashiers and they did not have to be suspicions of one another. With such family unity, working like one, the business would soon generate a great deal of money. Once there was money, the owners could expand their business. At that time, it was a fashionable thing to have many branch businesses, with the desire to achieve as many as the stars in the sky.

The branch businesses also adopted the model of a shop in front of the mill. This arrangement, however, gradually proved inappropriate for some trades. The making of cloth soles for shoes, for example, could be done just about anywhere. Why should that part of the trade be crammed into the expensive store? If a less

This was a husband-and-wife shoe store. Different types of shoes hang on the wall.

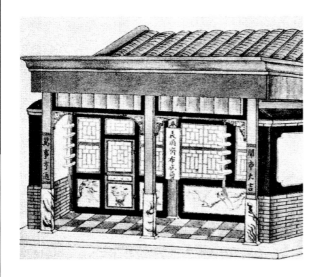

Yishenzhai, a workshop specializing in making soles for cloth shoes.

The Neiliansheng Shoe Store enjoyed a great reputation. Today, the store can still be found at Dashilan, Qianmen, Beijing.

expensive place was used as the workshop, not only would it be economical but it would also be easier to control the quality in a uniform way. As a result, sole making workshops appeared in the villages outside Guangqumen Gate. But for expensive shoe stores, such as Neiliansheng, it was necessary to have a special supplier of soles to ensure quality and therefore the reputation of the store. The most famous product from Neiliansheng was cloth soles for shoes. First, brand new white cloth was pasted together layer upon layer. And each layer was pressed hard and flat. When stitching the many layers of pasted cloth together, the best jute thread from Wenzhou was used. For every square inch, there needed to be eighty-one stitches or more. After stitching, the soles were soaked in water at 80-100oC and then wrapped in a

A shop sign hanging high outside a carpet and tapestry store.

thick cotton quilt for steaming. Once the soles had become soft, they were beaten flat, shaped and dried. Obviously, such a process required specialized workshops producing cloth soles on a contract basis. Individual villagers were just not qualified to make them.

Along with the progress of time, the small workshop production with a store in front of a mill became unable to resist the impact of mechanized commercial economy, and thus such stores receded into the legacy of history.

Not all of the operation experiences from olden times, however, are completely obsolete. If new concepts and ideas are applied, some of the production skills can still serve the new era.

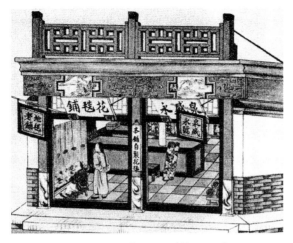

At the Quanshengyong Carpet and Tapestry Store, carpets were made right inside the shop to indicate that everything was genuinely "homemade."

A cotton-fluffing stand for making the insides of a cotton quilt.

Making cloisonne enamel -- a famous Chinese art and craft product.

A cloth dyeing workshop.

Workers casting iron to make woks in a makeshift wok factory.

"We're Handicraft Men!"

In introducing Xu Chengbei, a publisher of one of his works says: "Born to be disarmed and happy-go-lucky, with an exceptionally wide range of interests, keen on making friends and dedicated to writing. Play is work and work is play. This is Xue Chengbei."

In the past, people in the trades mostly learned from their fathers and then passed the skill on to their children. And in most cases, they loved what they did and made a living out of their skills. These days, few people work in the same profession throughout their entire working life. In my lifetime, I have changed jobs twice, once passively and at another time on my own accord. Both my parents were fairly well-known journalists and from my childhood I desired to go into their profession. Unfortunately, during the Anti-rightist Campaign of 1958, both of them were labeled "rightists." In choosing my own profession, I had to switch to opera script writing, which marked a turn from journalism to operas that dealt only with ancient characters. The second change of jobs took place in the early 1980s. Then I was working as a playwright for the China Peking Opera Troupe, but the development of the reform and opening up program led to a system of contracting by the troupe. Actors and actresses were busy performing in privately-arranged commercial shows, leaving playwrights in a useless position. So I decided to turn my attention to academic studies of Peking opera and I am still doing this today. I wonder whether this change of jobs was "from something old to something new" or vice versa? I think it belongs in the category of changing "from the old to the new," because the decline of opera performances in the new historic era is a result of the change of times, and thus the corrosion of the soil for writing play scripts was inevitable. Peking opera, however, embodies rich and profound cultural legacies that are rare in the opera circles of China today. It would be a great pity if no theoretical studies are made of this unique art form. That is why, for years, I have persevered in doing such studies, although my "new profession" is not the same as the "new profession" engaged in by some comic drama actors.

Generally speaking, the old trades and professions in an old city were determined by the lifestyle and work of the old residents. Though some of the trades and professions have since disappeared, their legacy is inherent in the traditional type of labor. An important mission for men of letters in this new era is to add a sense of history and cultural connotation to the new trades and professions.

One trade that has totally disappeared is canopy making. In olden times, canopies consisted of reed mats or cloth. Reed mats were used to build canopies in the courtyards of quadrangle houses. There was a great market for this trade in old Beijing. Wealthy people at that time believed that the only proper place for

Sign for a canopy or shed-making business. When a person of position or wealth died, "roadside sacrificial pavilions" would be built along the way his bier was taken.

Dengshikou or the Lantern Market Entrance had a cluster of lantern making businesses.

Lanterns hanging outside Wenshengzhai Store -- an established painting establishment for lanterns.

people to die was in their own homes. And so all memorial services were conducted at home under a canopy. To show off their wealth and social position, these families also had huge archways, a drum tower and a bell tower built outside the gate to their residences. The bell tolled and the drum was beaten to greet and send off guests who came to attend a memorial service. There were also cloth canopies. According to one story, when Emperor Qianlong went out of the palace to offer sacrifices to a god or to pay a visit to his ancestral tombs, cloth canopies were erected along the way in order to house the military command office, the imperial throne, the official flag and the tent residence. Each kind of canopy had its distinctive use at the beginning, but gradually the distinctions vanished. Middle-class families also erected canopies when they hosted celebrations. The canopies kept warmth inside and warded off heat in summer. Glass window panes were furnished along the four walls of the canopies and they were decorated with colorful eaves of various kinds. In

fact, the building of a funeral canopy better demonstrated the skills of the builder than the building of one for a happy occasion. Outside the funeral service canopy, a terrace, a Buddhist scripture tower and a sacrificial shed had to be erected as part of the deal. The difficulties involved were thus not very hard to imagine.

The top of the gate tower at Qianmen was brought down by cannon shots of the eight allied Western powers.

Another trade at that time was the making of colorful lanterns. From the Tang and Song dynasties onward, it was the custom for people to "watch lanterns" during the Lantern Festival and the scale of this activity became grander and grander. Today, a place in the East District of Beijing is still known as Dengshikou, or the Lantern Market Entrance, which is said to be the location of lantern

A "roadside sacrificial pavilion" of a minor official, such as a railway bureau chief, was audaciously erected in front of Tiananmen Rostrum during the years of the Republic (1911-49).

shows during the Ming and Qing dynasties. After the overthrow of the Qing Dynasty, nine lotus-shaped lanterns with colored balls and tassels were hung in the temple near the Lantern Market Entrance from the 12th to the 16th day of the first lunar month.

These two trades -- canopy building and lantern making -- once experienced a sorrowful "merging." Over a hundred years ago, the army of the eight allied Western powers marched into Beijing. Negotiations resulted in the signing of a humiliating peace treaty. In its wake, Empress Dowager Cixi and Emperor Guangxi returned from Xian where they had fled from Beijing aboard a train (the locomotive still carried a dragon flag at the time). In returning to the Forbidden City, they had to pass Qianmen but the gate tower,

Funeral service men carried the bier of Sun Yat-sen from the Green Cloud Temple in the western suburbs to the Summer Palace using "small carrying poles." Then they changed to "large carrying poles" to take the bier to the Qianmen Railway Station. The job was undertaken by the famous Sunrise Coffin Bearers.

called the Arrow Tower, had been shelled by the cannons of the eight allied troops. What to do? Someone came up with a so-called "good idea" -- bringing in skilled canopy builders and lantern makers to build a "new Arrow Tower" before the deadline. The artisans worked hard and the "new Arrow Tower" truly looked wonderful. The empress and emperor went through the gate, without anyone daring to expose the shameful sham.

When someone became deceased in a prominent family, a solemn funeral was inevitable. In the first volume of *The Old Beijing*, I wrote about the funeral of the famous Peking opera actor Yang Xiaolou, during which virtually the entire city turned out to watch. The organization that oversaw the bearers of coffins, who were called the Sunrise Coffin Bearers, was originally located near the subway station at Xidan, where the Chang'an Theater was built in 1937. In 1929, when the "grand ceremony to transfer Sun Yat-sen's bier for burial in Nanjing" was held, the service was performed by the Sunrise Coffin Bearers. At three in the morning on that day, they first went to the Green Cloud Temple to take Sun Yat-sen's corpse to the Summer Palace where they used the largest size of carrying poles to take the bier into the city through Xizhimen Gate, all the way to the Qianmen Railway Station, where they put the bier on a train bound for Nanjing. From the Summer Palace to the train station, 300,000 Beijing residents came to bid farewell to the founder of the Republic. Such a moving scene was unprecedented and would not be repeated in the future. It was a piece of good luck for the people engaged in this "old trade." If someone ever writes a book on the history of coffin carrying, this episode should not be left out.

In olden times, Caishikou (Vegetable Market Entrance) was the execution ground. It was important for the executioner to be highly skillful, so that with the fall of his sword, the head of the man condemned to death would roll off, instead of hanging loose on the man's shoulders. To ensure a "quick death," families of those to be executed would "bribe" the executioner. There used to be one most cruel punishment: cut the man sentenced to death three thousand times with a knife before he was allowed to die. If the person died before all the cutting and stabbing were finished, it

Handicrafts men selling their stone sculptures on the Great Wall.

A shoe repairer.

meant that the executioner did not do the job skillfully enough. And he would be penalized for such a mistake.

There were too many old trades and professions to speak of and often it is quite hard to get anyone to describe them all.

People live in greatest concentration in the urban areas and this is where the different trades first began to appear. Some of these grew in size and scale, while others gradually declined or even totally vanished. The change provides much food for thought. Ordinarily speaking, the old trades were mostly men's handicraft jobs. Though I have never tried any of the professions described above, their skills and the dedication and whole heartedness of the people in them are not difficult for me to understand. This is because what those people did and the play writing for Peking operas that I have done both fall into the realm of arts and handicrafts. Both demand a clear mind and a dexterous hand, in addition to a good understanding of the rules of the heart. Though I no longer write opera scripts, the rules and principles I used to follow closely in my writing career still nourish my heart and my mind and exert their impact on my writing. As we are increasingly coming in contact with hi-tech industries these days, it is important sometimes to return, even if just for a short time, to jobs in the handicraft trades so as to regain the flavor of life and realize the integration of mind and heart.

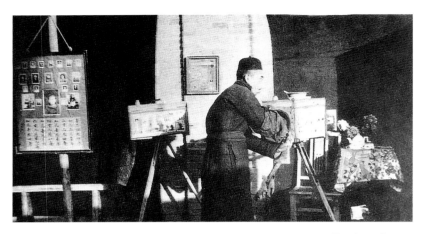

Early photo-graphers used cameras as big as chests. Sunlight was their lighting. All the photographic materials came from abroad.

A dentist's office in the 1940s.

Passion for Paintings

Take a stroll among the antique stands along the street and you might discover some valuable old paintings and calligraphic works among the snuff bottles, hand-warmers, bracelets, imperial court beads, bottles, jugs and vases.

If they had room, the old residents in Beijing would usually hang one or two works of "painting or calligraphy" on their walls. Of course every dynasty and historical period had its "painters and calligraphers whose works were in great demand," but the people of Beijing preferred works from a certain period in the "earlier dynasties." This seemed an inbred trait of the people in old Beijing. Indeed, sometimes, there was an interesting story behind an "old piece of calligraphic work or a painting".

Of course, there was the case of "discerning eyes discovering a treasure". Take the example of Ma Lianliang, a noted Peking opera superstar, who accompanied a friend of his to see a house. They went to see the house with the intention of buying it. To Mr. Ma's great surprise, he discovered on the wall of the house portraits of thirteen former Peking opera superstars.

Quietly Mr. Ma told this to his friend who quickly decided to buy the house on the precondition that the owner would not move the portraits out. After the deal was reached, Mr. Ma printed 10,000 pictures from the portraits and distributed them among his friends in the Peking opera circles to the delight of them all.

Speaking of old calligraphic works and paintings, mention must be made of a place called Liulichang Street that was a trading location for these art works. Located in the eastern part of Xuanwu District, the street was only 400 meters long and 8 meters wide. But the short and narrow street was flanked by many antique stores such as Rongbaozhai Studio, Four-treasure House, Xiguge Pavilion and

Liulichang Street is where the antique stores and shops of old paintings and calligraphy are, such as the Rongbaozhai Studio, and Xiguge Pavilion, as well as antique stands.

Living rooms in respectful houses without exception were hung with paintings and calligraphic works.

Signs for a shop carrying painting brushes, paper and ink.

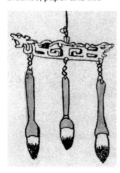

Qingyuntang Studio. If one ever set foot there, they would find it hard to pull away from the place. So in a way, it was a street that one could never walk to the end of.

The old art works were closely associated with the environment where they were found. In front of the wall on which paintings and calligraphic works were hung, there was usually a long table that provided the base for a clock and vases to holding things such as feather dusters. In front of the long table would be a square table called the "eight immortals' table," which was adorned with a tea set. Each side of the table would have an old-fashioned armchair with a beautiful cushion. So you can see that everything followed a set pattern. Because of these customs and habits, the trade related to paintings and calligraphic works developed, including the materials from brushes to ink and from xuan paper and ink slabs to silk for mounting the paintings. The diversification of mounting techniques and skills for appraising and evaluating cultural relics all had their place in society. These trades were mostly operated from small workshops managed by individuals who kept contact with each other on a one-to-one basis and did their business in closed chambers. Everything at the time seemed so mysterious.

When literati paintings and calligraphic works entered the homes of Beijing residents, it gradually elevated the cultural attainment of Beijing as a city. For example, when friends visited each other, after they were offered a cup of tea, they would hold the tea cup in hand and examine the surroundings. The pillars and beams of the living room would not change, but the maid might be a new person. All of this,

Opera pictures were a kind of traditional woodblock print. The print above features the opera known as *Punishing the Princess* and the lower one is from *Intercepting Three Times.*

however, was not what the guest wanted to pay attention to. What a guest was most interested in were the paintings and calligraphic works on the wall. If the host was a "middle-class" Beijinger or a person above that position, his total collection would be much more than what he displayed on the wall. Such collections were not only the pride of the owner but also what his friends were interested in. If the guest found that the paintings and calligraphic works on the wall were not what he had seen last time, this would be where the conversation began. No matter what urgent issue the guest had come to discuss with his host, their conversation would begin with a discussion of the paintings whenever something as conspicuous as a change of paintings on the wall in the living room had taken place. They would make a long "detour" before they moved on to the real topic for the day. This "patient characteristic" of people in old Beijing was such that you can even say they cared more for art than anything else, even

Fuchengzhai Painted Fan Studio that specialized in selling all kinds of palace fans, folding fans, etc. The fans were painted with flowers, birds, insects, fish, mountains, rivers and human figures.

Artisans busy in a painting mounting workshop.

if their houses were on fire.

Despite all the positive features of old paintings and calligraphic works, there were simply too many of these works in old Beijing. Those who painted for sale constituted the mainstream of the world of fine art, as they day after day mass-produced paintings similar in concept, subject matter, composition and color and ink. Painters like this no longer had anything to do with artistic creativity. Just think what kind of old paintings and calligraphic works can reflect history? I believe painters must pay attention to the cultivation of their own characters. Only then can their works reflect things that are larger than life and stand above the ordinary. Such painters have been and are many in the world of fine arts in China.

Stands of paintings on South Xinhua Street only accommodated the needs of ordinary citizens and normally did not sell paintings by famous artists.

The sign of the Runguzhai Painting Mounting Studio that specialized in reproducing paintings and calligraphic works of either famous or old-generation artists.

These four characters, meaning "mixed feelings of grief and joy", were written by master monk Hong Yi just before his death.

A very typical example is the work of Hong Yi, an outstanding Buddhist monk-calligrapher. Before he breathed his last, he wrote down four characters meaning "mixed feelings of grief and joy". Though the strokes suggested his hands shook as he wrote them, it is obvious he wrote with determination in the heart. These four characters of his are a brilliant piece of work that is to ever illuminate and not to be repeated in man's history. It really should be regarded as a fine example of the "unity of man and heaven" as well as a true "reflections of history".

First built during the Ming Dynasty and then expanded during the Qing Dynasty, the Hall of Celestial and Terrestrial Union sits on the axle in the Forbidden City where the twenty-five precious imperial seals that symbolized the power of the emperor were kept.

A glazed tile factory producing special tiles for palaces and temples. The picture shows decorative tiles for house ridges and gateway roofs.

59. ● TIEN-TSIN. - Joueurs et Chanteurs Chinois

The picture shows a band in front of Liu Jiesan's studio.

The Xishiku Cathedral in the West District of Beijing. When Empress Dowager Cixi was expanding the West Garden, she did not want people from the bell tower of the nearby cathedral to look into the imperial garden, so she appropriated money to give to French missionaries so that they would relocate their church. That was how the cathedral came to be where it is and why it grew into the largest Catholic church in Beijing.

Chapter 4
Both Old and New

Fold the hands and make a bow -- the typical way of greeting people on the Spring Festival in olden times.

At the Spring Festival

The old city of Beijing was always full of noise, a combination of human voices, peddlers' shouting in hawking their wares, and the sounds of horses and vehicles. As people were accustomed to the noise of the old Beijing, they naturally created more noise when they celebrated any festival.

Traditionally, the Spring Festival, Dragon Boat Festival and Mid-autumn Festival were the three most important occasions for celebration. And among these three, the Spring Festival was the most celebrated holiday. The question here is: where did all the noises of the Spring Festival come from?

The most noise came on the Spring Festival Eve. A month before the festival, people in Beijing were already busy shopping and preparing the things needed for the occasion. According to a popular rhyme: "The New Year is arriving and everything should look new. Girls want clothes of beautiful colors, boys buy firecrackers, the old lady needs a pair of felt shoes and the old man wants a felt hat to make him look good? According to another rhyme: "Buy melon-shaped maltose on the 23rd day (of the last month on the lunar calendar), write spring couplets to put on the door on the 24th, give the house a thorough cleaning on the 25th, go and buy meat on the 26th, slaughter chickens on the 27th, ferment dough for making pastry on the 28th. " Then when the last day before the Spring Festival arrived, people calmed down. They slept late in the morning and took a nap in the afternoon, all in anticipation of the New Year dinner that night.

The East Church at Bamiancao remains vivid among my childhood recollections.

On the last night of the year, the voices of the Spring Festival could be heard loud and clear. And the voices were a chorus of firecrackers, chopping meat on a chopping board and the crisp clacking of the abacuses as shops and stores finished the final accounts of the year. The air became permeated with the smell of

Streets in old Beijing before the Spring Festival were a scene of hustle and bustle, as people busily shopped, sold, loudly hawked their goods and heatedly bargained. In addition, there was the jingling of bells from rickshaws.

Shortly before the Spring Festival, temples and monasteries were already permeated with a happy and peaceful holiday atmosphere.

gunpowder from the firecrackers whose thundering sound drowned the city in a festival mood. Kids set off their firecrackers in the courtyard and the smallest of them were called "tiny whips." These were braided together -- 500 or even 1,000 of them. Bolder boys were more interested in the double-bang and loud-explosive types of firecrackers. Girls found joy in setting off fireworks that rose above the houses and were seen by pedestrians in the street.

Almost every home prepared dumplings to be had early on the New Year's Day as a symbol of family reunion. These were made on the last night of the year by mincing the meat on a chopping board.

There is a moving story according to which, a woman is alone at home on the eve of the Spring Festival as her husband has to hide himself away from creditors. When she hears the sound of mincing meat on the chopping board in neighboring houses, she can no longer hold back her tears. At the end, she decides to chop her board even there is no meat. As she works, her tears drop on the chopping board. And so she goes on chopping her fallen tears.

In shops and stores, the final counting was important as people wanted to know how much money they had made or lost during the year so that they could decide on how many shop assistants they could hire in the coming year. If the count proved to be in the red, the owner would have to hire fewer people. In having the last meal of the year, the owner would pick up a steamed dumpling and place it in the bowl of the assistant as a way of telling him that he would not be hired again in the coming year.

After midnight, this melding of three kinds of noises would begin to subside. Family members would gather around the stove, listening to the most senior person tell of the past events in the family. Those relatively old members would have heard the tales before, but still they needed to help the kids hear these tales. Old Beijingers never wanted to forget their roots and repeating the family history made them cool-headed. Near the stove would be a mahjong table surrounded by the middle-aged family members who by now no longer had the excitement of the first few hours of the

Young apprentices and child laborers were fearful that they might not be hired again for the coming year.

Men without much work to do gathered together to while away their time.

Before the Spring Festival, people pasted up prints of door gods in the hope that monsters and misfortunes would be kept away and that the whole family would stay happy and safe in the coming year.

night and could only manage to continue the game mechanically. When the day was about to break, the most senior member of the family would dismiss the whole-night vigil by saying: "Ok, we'll stop here." Members now went back to their own rooms and the quadrangle house quieted down. Soon snoring would be heard.

The learned owner of a quadrangle house might go into his study after midnight to write spring couplets, for he knew that in the morning people in the entire lane would come out and read the spring couplets on the doors of each home in order to see which family had the best ones, both in terms of the choice of words and the style of writing. They would also check to see which spring couplet best complimented the door of which house. The most hot-tempered people would not wait for daybreak, but would carry a lamp to read the couplets. Apparently, there was some kind of competition going on.

After a whole night of activity, people did not usually go out visiting on the first day of the Spring Festival.

On the eve of the Spring Festival, all doors were closed. Only snowflakes quietly descended on the stone drums in front of traditional houses.

Snow had stopped and the sun came out. Family members, old and young, began to visit their relatives to offer good wishes.

No matter how busy people were during the Spring Festival, they would not forget to light incense in front of the god of good fortune.

China has been a country of ceremony and propriety since ancient times. Classics dealing with the proper way to conduct oneself are too many for anyone to read all of them.

It was a day for recovering. On the second day, no one, whether old or young, would stay at home anymore. This was the day to visit relatives and friends and to greet each other with good wishes. People going on holiday visits did not go empty-handed. Cakes and pastries were the most common gifts. In the beginning, each family bought some of these, but soon the gifts began to change hands and the same things were passed from one house to another. After several rounds of exchange, the holiday would be almost over.

In old Beijing, the Spring Festival was not a time for hard thinking, but it was a time of uninhibited eating, drinking and playing. Old Beijing was a consumer's city. During normal days, the atmosphere was rather relaxed and the pace was not quick. As if this was not enough, people totally relaxed during the Spring Festival. This holiday was a result of the rural economy, as it came when the year's farming and harvesting were completed. Farmers put aside their tools for a rest and people in the urban areas joined them in this process of relaxation. In fact, the urban people were more relaxed than the farmers.

Since the founding of the People's Republic in

CHINESE ETIQUETTE

1949, many modern holidays have been introduced, but each person has his own choice holiday. This may not be a bad thing. Today's society is a pluralistic one. Why not many holidays? People are more and more carried away by their pursuit of a modern life with its quickening steps, but they may want to return to an old holiday like the Spring Festival for a change. And the more traditional, the better. If they can hear the noises of the past spring festivals, it will be all the more enjoyable.

When running into each other during the Spring Festival, people bowed with folded hands. They also exchanged pleasantries for the occasion.

The Squeaking Push Barrows

Push barrows used to be seen throughout China. In fact, they were still available in Beijing in the 1950s.

Whenever there was a drought or flood some one hundred years ago, squeaking barrows could be heard and seen traveling along the paths outside Beijing, headed for the city. The barrow pushers were mostly farmers from the disaster-stricken Hebei and Shandong provinces where they would only have starved to death if they continued to stay at home. On these barrows were, in most cases, boys who were the lifeline of the family. Wives and daughters might be trailing behind the barrow or simply struggling at home.

Changes in the means of transportation in Beijing during the 20th century have been quick and frequent. First there were the rickshaws, each pulled by a man in the front. They were either hired by people from the middle class on a monthly basis or served anybody who needed to go for a ride. Later, tricycles appeared. Like rickshaws they carried random passengers or were

Though simply made, push barrows were quite useful as they could carry both people and goods.

A mule-pulled cart with an elaborate canopy in old Beijing.

With a smaller canopy, an open cart was turned into a sedan cart, often used by women and opera stars.

A government-run cart service. The flag with the pattern of a dragon on it was a sign of the importance of the business.

A post station during the Qing Dynasty -- popularly called a roadside inn.

contracted out month by month. Gradually they replaced the man-pulled rickshaws.

Roads in Beijing were widened and asphalt surfaces were applied to them. Now came private cars. Apart from officials in the government and members of the military, the first private car owners in old Beijing included famous Peking opera superstars such as Mei Lanfang and Shang Xiaoyun. Shang's car had a very special horn so that when his driver pressed it, his fans could tell it was his car coming and they would

A ferry boat in suburban Beijing.

A rickshaw and a soft sedan chair.

say: "Let's make way. Haven't you heard? Mr. Shang is coming!"

Later, buses made their way onto the street. Those who were traveling from Xizhimen to Tsinghua and Peking universities could now ride in buses. But the buses at first were poor and clumsy monsters driven by coal-burning boilers attached to the back of each vehicle. The smoke was heavy and the buses were slow.

But automotive improvement had been fast. Very soon, brand-name vehicles from foreign countries were running around the streets of Beijing.

Trams also were seen on the street. As these had jingling bells, people referred to them as "dingdang

Rickshaw pullers were mostly bankrupt farmers who worked from early morning to late into the night in order to eke out a living.

One of the earliest private cars in old Beijing.

The bells of trams produced a jingling sound and residents in old Beijing referred to them as "dingdang buses."

buses." What was most difficult to imagine was that locomotives would pull a train into Beijing.

The city wall in Beijing was built following strict rules with gates and towers well arranged on all four sides. Trains certainly could not be allowed to go into the city through the city gates or under the towers! And if they were allowed into the city, wouldn't the century-long imperial atmosphere and environment be destroyed by these monsters? Still they finally made their way into the heart of the city and openings began to appear on the city walls. The chugging of the trains now shook the ancient city of Beijing. Once the trains were admitted, two railway stations went up near Qianmen in the center of the city: one in the west and the other in the east. All of this was the work of the time. Though it was a much difficult job for the trains to be admitted into the city, when they left the inner city district years later, all was very quiet.

I remember seeing a set of photos of Beijing in the 1940s: Tricycles, rickshaws and pedestrians were all traveling quickly, but they moved on the left-hand side

A tram service went through the embassy district in old Beijing.

A train arrived in Beijing through an opening in the city wall, causing many of the subjects of the Qing emperor to come out and watch with great curiosity.

Beijing Railway Station in the 1920s.

When Empress Dowager Cixi went to Shenyang, she traveled in a special train. The imperial kitchen alone took a whole carriage. But when the subjects of the Qing royal family traveled along the rails, they could only ride in this kind of third-class carriage.

of the street, just the opposite of what is permitted today. I cannot help wondering when people switched from the rule of traveling on the left to right? I asked many veteran residents about the matter but no one had the answer until an octogenarian said: "The change took place between 1925 and 1930. The left rule was German and the switch was from the German practice to the American practice." He added, "I find the change scientific."

From 1925 to 1930, vehicles in Beijing traveled on the left side of the road following a German practice. In 1930, the rule was changed and vehicles began to go along the right side.

The Emperor Called

Striking clocks were among the first things introduced into China from the West. They came as a great surprise to the emperor, empresses and court ministers.

Cultural exchanges between China and the West began with the exchange of souvenirs, such as striking clocks and music boxes. These small things were so delicate and cute that Empress Dowager Cixi was really surprised and fascinated. Later, a woman oil painter from the Western world came to Beijing and the empress agreed to have her do a portrait. The empress sat for several hours but when the painting was done she did not feel happy about it, for she found the color used for her was too dark, and she believed that the painting made her look ugly. Still later, automobiles and trains arrived in Beijing. Though happy when riding in a car, the empress was not satisfied that the car driver sat in front of her. She wanted the driver to kneel behind her and manage the car from there. Only in that way would things proper and in conformity with tradition! As for trains, she was against them from the

Foreign tourists making sketches in a small town attracted local people to come and look. Some even climbed to the house roof in order to get a closer look at the foreigners.

beginning. The empress was especially angry that when the trains entered Beijing through a section of the city wall that had to be taken down: "To open the city wall means the leaking out of the imperial air of the Great Qing!" Soon afterward, however, Wu Liqing, a capitalist widely known in Beijing and Tianjin, invited her and Emperor Guangxu to ride in a special train to Tianjin so as to "have fun." Both sides of this special train were painted with flying dragons and phoenixes in sparkling gold color, and the coach was complete with all the luxurious facilities. The empress was said to have fully enjoyed herself on this train and so her opposition to their entering Beijing "softened."

The footsteps of history were, after all, not made

because rulers "softened their opposition." Interestingly, it was at her birthday celebration that the great power of a current of electricity gave her a real surprise. In the Summer Palace, colorful lamp bulbs were hung out on all scenic spots and roads and they proved to be much better than lanterns dimly illuminated by candles. Thus electricity easily came into people's lives in Beijing.

It was a Westerner who first discovered electricity, understood its strength and then made use of it in daily life and production. After the imperialist powers invaded China, electricity was introduced in their wake. But it first was provided for the royal family and it would be a long time before it was applied to produc-

The Summer Palace a hundred years ago.

tion in China.

Next, the telephone appeared in Beijing. And the first houses to have this convenience were, of course, the Forbidden City and the imperial palaces. According to historical documents, switchboards were installed in the office area of the Forbidden City and the living quarters. Each switchboard was connected with phone sets in such places as the outer palace gate and inner palace gates. If someone came for a visit or for any other matter, the eunuch on duty no longer had to run, but simply used the phone to report to the right member in the royal family or the right official. Besides, this greatly sped up things.

These telephone sets first appeared in China in the 1920s and could still be seen in rural areas in the 1960s.

I have always thought the aides of the emperors and princes must have been very resistant to telephones. Emperors and princes were used to hearing servants reply with a loud "yes, yes," which gave them a sense of mighty power. Why should the efficiency of doing things be that important?

Slowly, the telephone service extended to the upper classes of society in the urban districts. The telephone bureau in Beijing was established and the nobility with telephones at home was listed in a telephone directory. According to one story, after the Revolution of 1911 that overthrew the rule of the Qing Dynasty,

the deposed Emperor Puyi with the reign title of Xuantong one day saw the name of prominent scholar, Hu Shi, in a copy of the telephone directory at the palace. (After his abdication, the emperor was allowed to continue to live in the Forbidden City for more than ten years -- translator) So he called Hu Shi, who happened to be at home and answered the call. Hearing a reply from the other end, the last emperor waited a little while but eventually let the man at the other end know that he was Emperor Xuantong. I have always wondered which term the emperor used in addressing himself. Did he say "I, the sovereign" or simply "I"? This could be an interesting topic for a psychological study. In the 1960s, my mother and the last emperor were both members of the National Committee of the Chinese People's Political Consultative Conference and I had meals with him at the same table of the canteen. At the time, I was already a Peking opera fan and sometimes teased him by using the term "I, the sovereign" to refer to myself, which caused him to be rather perplexed. At the time I was still in my late teens. Though I had already heard the story about his calling up Hu Shi, I did not dare to ask him which term he had used during the phone call. What a great pity!

Now to return to the last emperor's call to Hu Shi. When Hu Shi heard it was the emperor, he was taken by surprise. The emperor proposed that they meet and Hu Shi went to the palace at the appointed time. He bowed instead of kneeling and started the conversation with the emperor by referring to a book that lay on the emperor's table. They talked leisurely about "culture" and then Hu Shi politely took his leave.

It was several years later before electricity reached ordinary homes in Beijing, first in the eastern part, then

Puyi, the last emperor, with his empress Wanrong.

in the western part, and then in the Xuanwu and Chongwen districts. Finally it reached the western suburbs where universities are clustered.

Erection of electricity poles eventually led to a network of electricity wires. What a fantastic thing when electricity wire went into every home—who could tell what kind of machine or device the wire was hooked onto! And once electricity injected power into machines, what kind of consequences there would be?

With electricity wires in place, electric current could not be stopped any more. And the power and might of electricity were simply much greater than ferocious animals!

Although it is something that cannot be seen physically, electricity ushered in a storm that shook Beijing, troubled by corruption and backwardness, and led the Chinese society, which had been in isolation and seclusion, onto a fast track of modernity.

Hu Shi, the noted scholar who received a call from the last emperor.

The last emperor, Puyi, enjoying a game of golf.

No Words Needed

Liu Zengfu took this graduation photo in 1937 at the Yiyuan Studio in Wangfujing, Beijing.

In *The Gathering of the Heroes*, Peking opera superstar Yang Xiaolou played the part of Third Lady Huang.

Professor and medical physiology specialist Liu Zengfu, who is 85 years old this year, was once a student at Tsinghua University but later became a superclass specialist on Peking opera. Isn't this rather contradictory? Isn't this interesting? But it is a hard fact. When in the university, he could only come into town on Saturday evenings. And once in town he always went to watch a Peking opera. He had to return to the university in the northwestern suburbs by early Monday morning so that he could attend a German class. Recalling his experience, he says that he once saw an advertisement announcing that Yang Xiaolou and Qian Baosen were going to stage *The Gathering of*

Heroes on Sunday evening. This really troubled him for he did not want to miss the German class. But then that Saturday, the German teacher said he was going to attend the wedding of a friend on Sunday evening and so it was going to be too difficult for him to return to the campus late in the evening once the wedding was over. He thus canceled the class the following Monday. Liu was beside himself with joy. "This was a god-sent opportunity for me to watch a good show!" When he entered the theater on Sunday evening, the person in front of him suddenly turned around and it turned out to be his German teacher! The teacher and student looked at each other and smiled. No words were needed.

Mr. Liu Zengfu in 1997.

Now you might think that the teacher and student might have ruined their academic careers because they were so mesmerized by Peking opera. Well I don't really know the situation with the teacher, but Liu turned out "a winner both in his academic studies and in his Peking opera interest." He worked in the medical field in Beijing until he retired, achieving many successes in his profession. Besides, he took his academic methodology for scientific research into his studies of Peking

Yanjing University in old Beijing.

Jingshi College in 1898. Later it became known as Peking University.

opera, assuming the position of chairman of the Beijing Society for the Study of the Yu (Shuyan) School and publishing a book titled *A Study of Peking Opera Masks*.

Speaking of schools and colleges in Beijing, men-

The first campus of Peking University -- the Red Building at Shatan in downtown Beijing.

tion must be made of the Peking and Tsinghua universities. Once I read that it was the activities of the president, professors and students at a certain time and in a certain environment that created the campus culture of Peking University. Specifically, "Pursuing the principle of freedom of thought and learning from the strong points of all others" was the position of Cai Yuanpei (1868-1940), the president of Peking University. Professors from this university formed the backbone of China's New Culture Movement that appeared after 1919, while it was the students from this campus who were the movers and shakers of the patriotic May 4th Movement of 1919. These three elements constituted the complete whole that is called the spirit of Peking University.

Because of my profession, I usually pay more attention to Peking University. Among several generations of graduates there, quite a few have been my lifelong friends. And anyone of them is topic of a long and interesting story.

Tsinghua University specialized in the study of natural science. People say that "Differences in profession make one feel worlds apart," but then there is Mr. Liu who has made a "very scientific" study of Peking opera. His professional field of study was medicine but "accidentally" he came in touch with Peking opera and his studies won the total respect of professionals in that field as well.

His successful study of Peking opera made him a crystallization of the fine qualities of both Tsinghua and Peking universities and allowed him to make up for the shortcomings of students and teachers of both places. With this achievement of his, how could he not be successful? Though Mr. Liu is just one example, from him we can certainly imagine what great schools of learning these two typical institutions must be.

Early student life on the campus of Tsinghua, under the pen of the noted Professor Pan Guangdan, was something like this: "Over two hundred students at the beginning and no more than six hundred at most at its peak lived in a former royal garden more than sixty hectares in size. There was enough space for living and playing. There were iron beds and rice stalk cushions, and four people shared one large room. The lakeside, the woods and the stone stools on the hill slope were ideal spots to read. The garden had plenty of flowers and trees, and the chrysanthemums alone had more than two hundred varieties." By Mr. Liu Zengfu's time, two students shared one room which was complete with cupboard and shelves. The old beds had been replaced with spring beds that could be taken apart easily. In winter, when outside temperatures dropped to

Tsinghua University was built in 1911 with the war indemnities that the Qing government paid to the United States. It began as a preparatory school for students going to study in the US. In 1925 it grew into a university, and in 1928 took the name of National Tsinghua University.

minus 20oC, one sweater was enough to keep one warm inside the bedrooms. Small shops on Chengfu Road outside the southern gate of the campus sold ice cream that was good and inexpensive. Did students relax with their studies under such comfortable conditions? Certainly not. Sa Benlan, who later became a noted physicist, never went for a visit of the Summer Palace nearby though he spent eight to nine years studying at Tsinghua! In reality, there were many hardworking students like him at Tsinghua.

Professors at Peking University did not need to worry about their living standards, for things were cheap and their salaries were high.

For a bag of wheat flour weighing twenty-two kilograms, it was only a little over three yuan. Half kilo of pork cost no more than a dozen cents. And an ordinary professor's monthly salary? At least 200 to 300 yuan. For a senior professor, the monthly pay could go well beyond 600 yuan.

It was said that many foreign girls took it as a matter of pride to be married to professors at Peking University. My grandfather (on my mother's side), who had been a student of biology in Japan, used to teach at Beijing Normal University and also took a second job at the Ministry of Education. With income from these two jobs, the family was soon able to buy a small quadrangle house near Shifuma Bridge inside the Hepingmen Gate. The whole family moved in. A cook, a maid and a footman were hired, and in addition a rickshaw was

A private school in old China.

Private schools consisted of family schools, free schools and boarding schools. Usually there was only one teacher at a private school, who taught students on a one-to-one basis. There were no hard rules as to the syllabus and term of studies.

hired on a monthly basis. Later my grandfather lost one of these jobs and began to experience a shortage of money. So he went back to his hometown of Suzhou, where after having nothing substantial to do for two to three years, he found a job as a high school master. Now he was well off again. I went into this with the intention of saying that teachers at the time enjoyed decent salaries and social positions.

Now, as Beijing is in the middle of a new development stage, my recollection of the past is meant to better understand the future.

The former residence of Lu Xun, a leading 20th century author, in Third West Lane, Kongmenkou, Beijing.

Rickshaw boys ran against wind and snow in order to make a living. It was not infrequent for old rickshaw pullers to drop dead in the street, under the double pressure of poverty and illness.

Posters on an archway

Peking, Railway Station 30.7.08.

As Western civilization cracked open the door of China, which had been closed to the outside world, rails were posted to the foot of the city wall of Beijing. Later they extended all the way into the heart of the imperial capital of Beijing. This was the cargo station near Qianmen.

The Museum of the Palace, Peiking.

故宫博物院

After the abdication of the last emperor and the founding of the Republic of China in 1911, the Forbidden City, which had been closed to ordinary citizens, was turned into the Palace Museum and opened to the public.

Editors' Note

Changes a city has undergone are an important part of the history of the development of a civilization. In publishing this series of books, we have been guided by one consideration, i.e., to give readers a brief history of some well-known Chinese cities by looking at some old sepia photos taken there and reading some remembrances with regard to those cities.

Not like conventional publications, each book of this series contains a large number of old photos selected to form a pictorial commentary on the text. This provides a good possibility for readers to learn about Chinese urban history, cultural evolution in urban society in a new perspective. It also enables readers to re-experience historical "vicissitudes" of those cities and relish feelings of urban folks of China in the modern times.

To better illustrate those cities, we have commissioned renowned writers who have not only lived in their respective cities for a long time but also have been known for their strong local writing style. Either in presenting a panoramic view of a city or depicting fate of men in street, their writings are always so natural yet full of feelings.

This series of books have been published originally in Chinese by Jiangsu Fine Art Publishing House. The English edition has been published jointly by the Foreign Languages Press and Jiangsu Fine Art Publishing House.

Foreign Languages Press
Oct.2000 Beijing

图书在版编目(CIP)数据

老北京:巷陌民风/徐城北著;黄友义译.—北京:外文出版社,2001.4
(老城市系列)
ISBN 7-119-02837-5

Ⅰ.老… Ⅱ.①徐… ②黄… Ⅲ.散文-作品集-中国-当代-英文 Ⅳ.I267
中国版本图书馆 CIP 数据核字(2001)第 18624 号

中文原版

选题策划	叶兆言　何兆兴　顾华明　速　加　杜　辛
主　　编	朱成梁
副 主 编	何兆兴
著　　文	徐城北
图片供稿	中国照片档案馆　张洪杰　刘　震　王建华
装帧设计	顾华明
责任编辑	何兆兴　杜　辛

英文版

策划编辑	兰佩瑾
翻　　译	黄友义　丛国玲
英文编辑	卓柯达
责任编辑	兰佩瑾

老北京·巷陌民风

ⓒ外文出版社
外文出版社出版
(中国北京百万庄大街 24 号)
邮政编码 100037
外文出版社网址:http://www.flp.com.cn
外文出版社电子信箱:info@flp.com.cn
　　　　　　　　　sales@flp.com.cn
利丰雅高制作(深圳)有限公司印刷
2001 年(大 32 开)第 1 版
2001 年第 1 版第 1 次印刷
(英文)
ISBN 7-119-02837-5/J·1564(外)
08000(精)

老城市

OLD CITY